You are also asking me questions, and I hear you; I answer that I cannot answer ... you must find out for yourself.

— Walt Whitman, *Song of Myself*

Reviews and comments

Soothing and stimulating at the same time, these very digestible "meditations" show how a secular writer can convey very timely and worthy messages without being quarrelsome. Kudos to Chris Highland for taking us down this pleasant path of wisdom and realism.

Linda LaScola, co-founder of The Clergy Project
co-author, *Caught in the Pulpit: Leaving Belief Behind*

Chris Highland does a wonderful job introducing the atheist perspective to an audience that may not otherwise seek it out. Without being confrontational, he raises important questions while helping readers understand that atheists are a vital part of their community.

Hemant Mehta, editor, FriendlyAtheist.com

I often meet good people who feel lost and lonely because they've lost faith, friends, or family or, worst of all, all three in one fell swoop … How grateful I am to introduce such wanderers to Chris Highland, a wise, compassionate guide who has blazed his own trail through the wilderness on the other side of faith.

Bart Campolo, Humanist Chaplain, U. of Cincinnati
host, Humanize Me podcast

While he may no longer be a believer, Chris Highland has not lost his pastor's heart. He continues to teach and challenge, to comfort the afflicted and afflict the comfortable, drawing on everyone from Henry Thoreau to Stevie Wonder. Taken to heart, this book will see walls come tumbling down, walls that keep us from one another.

Bob Ripley
author, *Life Beyond Belief: A Preacher's Deconversion*

This seminal work by Chris Highland is captivating, intriguing, and challenging. Each chapter is a gem in itself, and together they make for a powerful book by a very enlightened and savvy professional.

> **John S. Compere**, PhD; VP, The Clergy Project
> author, *Outgrowing Religion*

Gospel means "good news!" Chris Highland's *A Freethinker's Gospel* is indeed good news. In a time of chasms that divide, this is a book of bridges... [I]t models how clear commitment to a humanistic, naturalistic approach to life can walk hand-in-hand with genuine curiosity about differences of belief. Reading this collection felt like taking a walk through the fascinating and endlessly complex landscape of the Earth community with an amiable, knowledgeable, keen-eyed, open-minded, open-hearted companion and guide...

This book, like the natural world, calls you to linger. To pay attention... You'll experience moments that will elevate your spirit, take your breath away, fill you with a sense of wonder, and cause you to ask questions, reexamine your preconceptions, reflect, and dig deeper as you see possibilities you may have never before noticed – possibilities to build a bridge to a better world.

> **The Rev. Canon Charles Gibbs**, Episcopal
> Senior Partner, Catalyst for Peace Foundation
> Founding Executive Director, United Religions Initiative

I was particularly struck with [the] straight to the heart and straight to the point presentation.... [A] very nice mix of well crafted, substantive columns.

> **Laurence Cotton**, historian
> producer, *Frederick Law Olmsted: Designing America*

What I love about this book is that it truly — and intentionally — honors questions, not answers. Chris himself has lots of questions — and he is very comfortable not having answers for them ... Chris muses and reflects, wonders as he wanders. The essays are varied, inspiring, informative and creative. His gentle style builds bridges and opens doors with folks of many faiths, and those with no religious connection at all. He can raise thorny questions as well, which awakens a sharpness of vision and awareness. This book is a great companion for time alone, or for stimulating conversation with others.

Sara Vurek, Buddhist, Clinical Chaplain

Chris always inspires me with his ability to connect with everyone, no matter what their background or belief or where they are in their life. He has such a unique view on life as a religious leader who is open to all religions. I love how he encourages us to extend our bubbles of belief to include everyone.

Moji Javid, Director of Synagogue Engagement
Congregation Rodef Sholom

Chris Highland's ... articles are delightful and stimulating excursions for anyone interested in how beliefs affect the way we relate to each other. His genuine interest in the thoughts of others, and his willingness to describe his own, reveals a well-grounded sensibility that seeks to bridge the gaps between people divided by the beliefs or doubts that we happen to hold.

Jim Gronvold, former shelter counselor and administrator
author, *Pith & Piffle: overt verse*.

Pisgah Press was established in 2011 to publish and promote works of quality offering original ideas and insight into the human condition, the realm of knowledge, and the world around us.

Copyright © 2018 Chris Highland

Printed in the United States of America

Published by Pisgah Press, LLC
PO Box 9663, Asheville, NC 28815
www.pisgahpress.com

Photos of the author (cover, pp. 194, 226) by Carol Hovis
All other photos by Chris Highland
Cover photo: Water Rock Knob, Blue Ridge Parkway

All rights reserved. No part of this publication may be reproduced, stored in a retrieval system, or transmitted, in any form or by any means, electronic, mechanical, photocopying, recording, or otherwise, without the prior written permission of Pisgah Press, except in the case of quotations in critical articles or reviews.

Library of Congress Cataloging-in-Publication Data
Highland, Chris
A Freethinker's Gospel: Essays for a Sacred Secular World

Library of Congress Control Number: 2018955532

ISBN-13: 978-1942016397
Religion/Nature

First Edition
First Printing
October 2018

A Freethinker's Gospel

Essays for a Sacred Secular World

Chris Highland

Author of *Meditations of John Muir* and
My Address is a River

Contents

Introduction xi

1 Secular Devotion 1
2 Bubbles, Beliefs, and Religious Education 5
3 Giving Thanks 9
4 Adopting the Bethlehem Baby 13
5 The Good beyond Us and Them 17
6 When a Minister No Longer Believes 21
7 Holy Books 25
8 Ever Mindful of the Needs 29
9 Give Fire to the Dreams 33
10 Secular Prayers 37
11 One Nature Indivisible 41
12 I Can't Wait to See Heaven 45
13 Other Rivers 51
14 Nature of Humanism 55
15 Climbing Out of Hell 59
16 Secular Jesus 63
17 Bridges to and from Belief 69
18 Secular Holy Week 73
19 Awakening to Sabbath 77
20 Peeves, Goats, and the Faith of Children 81
21 Shoes On, Shoes Off 85
22 Children and Their Questions of Faith 89
23 Was Jesus Ever Wrong? 93
24 Welcoming People Not Like You 97
25 Faith Lessons from Frederick Law Olmsted 101
26 Rivers across the Religious Landscape 107
27 Here We Sit: 500 Years of Reformation 111

Contents

28 No Secular Crusades 115
29 "Blessed Are the Poor"? That Can't Be Right 119
30 Ingersoll: His Middle Name was Green 123
31 The Face of Nature 129
32 What Does it Mean to be a Religious Progressive? 133
33 The Interfaith Alternative 137
34 Seeing through Stevie Wonder's Eyes 141
35 Thoreau, Darwin, and Nature's Book 145
36 The Wisdom of Doubt 149
37 Fostering Contemplation 153
38 A Parable for Today 157
39 Is Your Family Divided by Faith? 161
40 Bridging the God-Gap 165
41 Francis of Assisi: Secular Saint? 169
42 Seeing What We Need to See 173
43 The Freethinking Gospel of Frances Wright 177
44 When Suffering Comes to the Door 181
45 Does Nature Care About Us? 187
46 Climbing Beyond Scripture 191
47 Theology for Beginners 195
48 Kitty Hawk, Curiosity, and an Ethic of Care 199
49 Proverbs from the Sea-Island Gullah 203
50 Walt Whitman, Chaplain 207
51 Facing Disasters, with Faith or without 211
52 So You Believe or Don't Believe—Then What? 215

Afterword: Seeking Truth with Lucretia Mott 221
About the Author 227

Crabtree Falls, Blue Ridge Mountains

Introduction

Here in the Blue Ridge Mountains of western North Carolina, nature is an open book. You not only read it; you lace up your boots and step inside. Living on the edge of the Blue Ridge Parkway, my wife Carol and I venture out into nature as much as possible, just as we habitually did during our years in the San Francisco Bay Area. On our walks and drives we always carry an ample amount of curiosity—what's around that bend? Where does that trail lead? What kind of bird is that? Literally hundreds of species of animals and plants are close neighbors, filling the pages of daily mountain life.

Not far away, through the hills and "hollers," passing whole forests of crosses, churches, and occasional Confederate flags, the Great Smoky Mountains National Park stretches like a great sanctuary with its 1,500 kinds of flowering plants, countless trails, and delightful waterfalls. It's the most visited park in the National Park system, but we don't have to go anywhere to sense that we live in the very heart of nature's wholly secular sanctuary ("secular" simply means this present world).

To a native West Coast person, the Southern Appalachians can be a little overwhelming. I'm used to verdant beauty and wild open spaces—but here in the Eastern Highlands, it seems every day I see some new bird or bug, flower or tree; bears, bobcats, turkeys, snakes, rabbits slither, scoot, or scurry by my door.

As naturalist John Burroughs observed, "One has only to sit down in the woods or the fields, or by the shore of the river or the lake, and nearly everything of interest will come round" (*A Sharp Lookout*, 1896). We don't have to be mountain climbers or Appalachian Trail through-hikers to be immersed in natural wonders.

With nature literally dropping by, I am constantly reminded of the delightful diversity that makes this land so wonderfully beautiful and interesting. That goes for the human inhabitants here, too, especially when it comes to backgrounds and beliefs. These differences and their challenges are fertile ground for the classes I teach and the books, blogs, and columns I write. I hope readers will find a taste of that natural harvest scattered through these pages.

Secular Shoes in the Bible Belt

How could a former minister who now wears the shoes of a freethinking humanist become perhaps the only avowedly non-religious person writing for the religion page of a newspaper anywhere? And in the Bible Belt?

In California, where Carol and I were active in interfaith work, our local newspaper carried a regular "sacred space" section, covering the Buddhist centers, activities at synagogues or mosques, news from Hindu retreats and Protestant, Catholic, and evangelical congregations. Religiously-based nonprofits were regularly highlighted as well. Our work led us to personal and professional connections with people of many faiths—including those organizations featured in "sacred space"—and since Carol served on the advisory board of the newspaper, we had some insight into the thinking of editors and publishers.

Even before we arrived in North Carolina I was reading the Asheville *Citizen-Times* online. I was impressed by the coverage of local issues as well as national stories (the paper is an affiliate of *USA Today*). At the time, the late Billy Graham's syndicated column "My Answer" appeared in the daily paper, but the Saturday religion section also caught my eye. Sharing a page with church announcements was a prominent weekly "Devotional" (as I saw it, more of a mini-sermon or Bible study), written by a local pastor.

A few months after our move, I contacted News Director Katie Wadington to propose a balance to the almost exclusively Christian content. As a long-time interfaith chaplain with ten books in print, now teaching courses on the history of early American Freethought at UNC Asheville's Reuter Center, I suggested that I could offer a sensitive presentation of issues concerning faith, based on my own naturalistic humanism but with no anti-religious slant. I made it very clear that I was not interested in replacing the devotional.

Katie put me in touch with Bruce Steele, the planning editor, and before long my columns were appearing each Saturday along with the pastor's reflections. In time, I was considered not a guest writer but a regular columnist. Given my name, and the fact that I was sharing my viewpoints from here in the highlands of WNC, what could be a better title than "Highland Views"?

Threads and Themes

The columns saunter across the landscapes of thought, searching for bridges—images, stories or creative ideas that might offer something relevant for readers with or without faith. My topics, secular and spiritual, range from "secular devotionals" on Francis of Assisi, Martin Luther, John Muir, Frances Wright, and others, to thoughts on biblical passages, verses from the Qur'an, Bhagavad Gita, the Tao, and the Dhammapada of Buddha. I also interview a diverse selection of clergy representing an array of traditions to hear and exchange ideas.

I frequently cycle back to the natural world both in words and photographs, reflecting my belief that nature is precious and primary, as well as my suspicion of superstitious or super-natural worldviews that distract our attention from "worldly matters" with promises of something better "up there"—above, behind, and beyond the observable, beyond reason and common sense. Disrespect for nature—including our secular world—can too easily devalue the natural, rational mind, and often goes hand in hand with disregarding those who recognize that the environment is our habitation, foundational and central to all life.

Through a virtual community of former and current religious leaders who no longer believe (The Clergy Project), as well as Americans United for Separation of Church and State, the American Humanist Association, and other non-theist groups, I also try to keep my finger on the pulse of the non-religious world—a pulse common to everyone. While I'm tempted at times to preach secular sermons (as I do in Unitarian congregations), I don't write columns as if I were a secular evangelist preaching a "Godless Gospel."

My purpose is not to "de-convert" anyone, but if someone is encouraged to consider reasonable alternatives to their beliefs, it may be helpful for them to read other points of view. Fear-based orthodoxy ("right opinion") discourages this kind of honest consideration; I hope through my unorthodox approach to present freethought as the "gospel" (good message) that it is.

An Invitation to Common Ground

My fundamental intent is positive, inviting, and educational. When a non-threatening freethinker approaches faith so as to open doors to new ideas rather than to smash the stained glass of unquestioning belief, we can create an opening for curiosity and an invitation to conversation.

Many of my readers are people of faith. One emailed my editor to say, "I am a person of faith, a church-goer, but nonetheless derive great benefit (and conversation topics) from reading Chris each week. Congratulations to both you and Chris for this highly intelligent, well-written addition to our great hometown paper." A Jewish reader wrote: "Great column–you are balancing out the fear-based religion of Billy Graham and others. Shalom." Yet another wrote: "Thank you for your courage in publishing such clear, well thought out (albeit controversial) common sense articles. Nice to experience 'thought freedom' so well articulated." And, after a presentation at a local, ecumenical housing complex, a woman came over to tell me—with a big smile—that she reads my columns "religiously."

Of course I have critics as well, here in the tightly-buckled Bible Belt and beyond. I'd be surprised, and disappointed, if I didn't. When a reader—critic or fan—thinks something I've written sounds too critical, or even "anti-faith," I urge them to remember: I have close friends and family who are people of faith, including a wife who's an ordained Presbyterian minister. They will be reading, too, and I want to encourage reflection as well as honest responses to what I write. In fact, Carol reads and comments on each weekly column before I submit it to my editor, and her suggestions and questions are invaluable.

My disappointments and disagreements with religion over the years have only spurred me to keep sharpening my questions and critiques. But while I speak with a sharp tongue, it is not a forked one. Some may not like the incisive issues I raise, but I suspect their faith can weather my "gentle style," as one person put it. If not … well, that's what the sports pages are for.

Chris Highland
Asheville, North Carolina
September, 2018

The pond at Connemara, Carl Sandburg's home in Flat Rock, NC

Dedication

In honor of Janet and Charlie Hovis

A Freethinker's Gospel

Essays for a Sacred Secular World

One
Secular Devotion

The intention of each of these essays is to present stories and reflections that may be of interest to both believers and nonbelievers. I write from a "satisfied secular" perspective to nudge readers to think a bit more deeply about issues of faith while considering alternative views of religious and non-religious experience. This essay, questioning the meaning of "devotion" and asking whether a nonbeliever can be devoted to higher principles, launched my newspaper column as it does this book.

A curious homeless woman sat by me in a free dining room one day and asked what religion I believed in. I smiled and told her I was an ordained minister, but in my role as a chaplain I was representing the compassion of the faith communities, the care of good people in the county. She was puzzled but seemed to appreciate that. I was curious too: "What is happening in your life—Anything we can do to help you?"

My wife Carol and I have been deeply involved with interfaith work for many years. Both of us have been ministers and chaplains. Between us, we have served as a nonprofit director, a shelter director, a teacher, a writer, and a housing manager. We have seen first-hand this simple truth in action: when faith communities and their friends practice the central ethics of their religion (love, goodness, a sense of justice), when they communicate and cooperate for the greater good, wonderful things can be done.

For many members of faith traditions, "devotion" means whole-hearted commitment to one faith, one church, synagogue, mosque, or temple, and one "true view" of God. A "devotional" can be a reflection on our lives too, can it not? Some might say the best prayer is action. Or, we could say, "doing unto others as we wish they do to us" is the whole point of any devotion.

We live in confusing times (understatement!). Culture wars and moral battle lines are drawn. It's much easier to build walls and defend them than it is to build bridges and beautify them. Does it always have to be Us and Them? There's so much to be done in our communities. As neighbors we can work together to do what is needed. We can, we often do, and we can do better.

The secular community cares about our shared world, too, since it's the only world we know for sure (secular means "this present world"). Seculars are not all anti-religious. We are already your neighbors, and maybe your friends and family. We are Americans too. The growing number of those who are unaffiliated with any one faith group (the "nones," including atheists, agnostics, freethinkers) don't wish to silence those who believe in other worlds—we simply want a voice at the table here and now, in this world.

Take for example that here in North Carolina someone like me is technically forbidden from holding public office. Our state constitution (Article VI, sec 8) says, "The following persons shall be disqualified for office: First, any person who shall deny the being of Almighty God."

Did you know that six other states also bar non-religious folks from public office? Does that sound fair? It doesn't sound like America, does it? (Though still on the books, the laws are unenforceable.)

Naturalist John Burroughs, a friend of both John Muir and Teddy Roosevelt, offered this curious bit of devotional reflection: "If we do not go to church so much as did our [parents], we go to the woods much more, and are much more inclined to make a temple of them than they were."

Naturalistic thinkers remind us of the great temple of nature, the cathedral of the wild spaces open to all, where folks of all creeds and none can gather to listen to a new "voice in the wilderness" calling out beyond our sectarian firewalls — the boundaries in our brains. Think of our National Parks.

Most of us who have left the "faith of our fathers and mothers" are not angry, anti-faith people who want to "take God out of schools," close churches, steal Christmas and ban the Bible. We have a curious devotion. We are devoted to curiosity and investigation, to seeking solutions to problems and issues that face us all, faith or no faith, this political party or that, this race or that, this gender or that. We know that freedom of thought, like "freedom of religion," also means freedom to choose no religion. Truth is, I'll defend your right to believe as you choose. Will you defend mine?

Like that "housing-challenged" woman in the free dining room that day, my curiosity is piqued: I wonder what would happen if people of faith peeked over the walls. I wonder what could happen if nonbelievers helped build those bridges that connect rather than divide — and what might happen if we were more devoted to each other, and our higher principles, than proving our point or winning an argument.

Two
Bubbles, Beliefs, and Religious Education

My religious education began in Sunday School, memorizing Bible passages. During evangelical years there were Bible studies each week and plenty of "godly" teachers to tell us what lessons we needed to learn from "God's Word." In college I ate up as much biblical studies, Greek language, and church history as I could. Seminary offered more in-depth exploration of scriptures and much more. But how is religion or any other form of spirituality taught in a meaningful way, especially as younger people lose interest? This chapter relates several hopeful stories — but also identifies some missing pieces, as people face their bubbles of belief.

I was invited to give an "Introduction to Humanism" for a Religious Studies class at the University of North Carolina—Asheville (UNCA). It's always a delight to present a positive secular point of view, especially among the next generation. Before I stood up to speak, the professor collected papers, and I remembered the relief I used to feel after long nights of study. Students were asked to name the spiritual communities they visited for their assignment, and it was great to hear the diversity: Catholic, Protestant, Greek Orthodox, Jewish, Sufi, Wiccan, Buddhist, and Bahá'í. It was encouraging to hear they had each made the effort to have face-to-face interviews with women and men representing these various beliefs, then stayed to observe their rituals and services. I sensed enthusiasm, maybe a touch of enlightenment, as the students named their chosen subjects. I was impressed, thinking, *There's hope for the world, and it starts here before my eyes.*

Having worked in multi-faith circles for more years than these students have been alive, I commended the instructor for her insightful assignment. For her this is simply a natural, rational way to teach this hot-potato subject of Religion. She told me the department doesn't teach Religion but rather *about* religion, which makes sense in a public university. Teachers have a challenging job presenting such an emotionally charged subject in an academic context, never quite sure how much a student's worldview has been shaped by family and faith. We could hope that by the time they reach college most women and men have been exposed to so much knowledge that they know there is much more to know. Yet the question is: are they ready for the practice of wisdom, a primary value in secular education?

Speak with just about anyone about faith and it becomes crystal clear that something is broken in religious education. Many of us were brought up in a bubble, and our beliefs float in that fragile sphere for a long time. Confronting, and fixing, what's broken is not about bursting anyone's bubble, including our own: it's about making choices. Good education trusts the mind, offering alternatives to choose from.

If we're taught to be fearful of anything or anyone outside our bubble-world, it can be extremely hard to take a "leap of reason" and think wisely, freely. In fact, extremism is born in these bubbles where it can quickly grow into fear-based violence—harming the brain, the body, and the world outside ourselves. We see this threat around the world—"over there"—but we can be blind to the smaller bubbles nearby, or in ourselves.

Those bubbles can be prison cells for some. I recall a powerful image from my jail chaplaincy years. Two inmates were housed in cells divided by a concrete wall. One was black, the other white. One young, the other a little older. When I walked up to the steel bars, both men came over to speak with me. They couldn't see each other, but both could see me. They told me they had been having a conversation about their disagreements over scriptural beliefs and sexual orientation; they voiced their different opinions as I quietly listened to both perspectives. As I prepared to leave, each man reached through the bars to shake my hand. Then, they reached around the wall and shook each other's hand, saying they would think about the other man's point of view.

That image has stayed with me—people learning from each other even through walls.

Just as prisons are bubbles where we put people who may not fit comfortably into the larger community sphere, our greatest punishment is self-imposed separation. We need to be aware when we keep some people away from others or try to bar some ideas from our heads.

Maybe the whole world is a big blue bubble (the earth is surely shaped like one) and the real illusion is that we are separate. Philosophers, mystics and others have suggested this. I'm not sure, but when I listened to those inmates or stood up to speak with those students about Humanism, I was looking into the eyes of the future. And those eyes were not bubbles.

Three
Giving Thanks

When holidays roll around, a majority of people assume that everyone celebrates or needs to celebrate. Most people think it's a sign of being a good citizen to "do the holidays" just like everyone else. This column was published near Thanksgiving so I decided to reflect on who gives thanks and why. Who or what do we thank? If it stirs up a conversation, great. If not, we're back to another holiday that pushes us to "take sides and defend." Let's hope we can talk about these things so we can all "celebrate" — if not together, at least with some understanding.

Autumn is a season for a lot of gratefulness. The beauty of trees and skies. Cool, crisp, star-lit nights. Migrating birds and sleeping bears. A time for many to gather with family for the national holiday. But how can someone without family be thankful? And how can someone without faith offer thanks? Good questions.

Thanksgiving is the perfect holiday for believers and unbelievers to celebrate. This shouldn't be too shocking, since a national day set aside for appreciation seems ideal for everyone regardless of religious belief. I hear the objections: "That makes no sense! We gather to give thanks to GOD! Holiday means HOLY-day, so if you don't believe, this day isn't for you!"

I hear you. But we're Americans too, so allow me to show some ways that secular citizens can still be thankful people. This may also be encouraging for non-religious neighbors who can often feel a little left out of celebrations.

If a person has no family, or is far from their family, they can still find someone to say thank you to, and something to be thankful for. They can thank their loved ones. They can thank people doing compassionate work—in nonprofits for example—for all the good done throughout the year. They can wave a "thank you" to a stranger simply for giving a parking space, for a friendly smile or for opening a door out of courtesy (this still happens!).

Freethinking people can always be thankful for freedom of speech, of thought, the freedom to not believe what someone else believes. This doesn't have to be an angry rejection. It can be a positive acknowledgement that liberty is a wonderful gift from our founders, our defenders, and all those who work to preserve our basic human rights.

We can't forget there are many who aren't feeling very grateful this time of year. Many of our neighbors are still unhoused, addicted, struggling to find support or anyone who cares. I lost both my parents in this darker time of year. It can be quite depressing. There are no magic words to make us or another person thankful. Yet, contentment is possible when the small things are appreciated—if we take the time to notice.

Simply breathe. Take a walk. Listen to the wind, the birds, the howl of coyotes, the babble of a baby. Be appreciative, and show it. Why not? Thank someone and they usually thank you right back. That's a gift, isn't it?

There is always something to be thankful for in nature. I take heart in the enthusiastic words of naturalist John Muir, who, in one day in the mountains, was delighted by three wild friends: a "restless fussy fly with gauzy wings," a bear who appeared as a "rugged boulder of energy," and a grasshopper that danced for him as a "crisp, electric spark of joy." At sundown, the weary mountaineer returned to camp and scribbled in his smoky journal, "Thank you, thank you all three for your quickening company. Heaven guide every wing and leg. Good-night friends three, good-night" (*My First Summer in the Sierra*).

"Ah-ha!" you might say. "See! He says 'heaven guide.' He was thankful to God." Well, yes, he was that too. Muir was a believer and he often spoke of the divine, of spiritual things. He had the Bible memorized. Yet, in his journals Muir made a startling statement: "No synonym for God is so perfect as Beauty … all is Beauty!" As for heaven, the wild Scotsman felt he was already sauntering the paths of paradise. He said that even the most fervent preacher might awaken in mountain beautyland and "fancy himself in heaven."

How can a person without faith in God or a holy book or heaven be thankful? How could they NOT be? Faith is not the only means of showing gratefulness. A deep breath, a silly dance, a smile for the beauty is enough, isn't it?

Whether we gather or not at Thanksgiving with family or friends or the wild things of the forests or mountains, the most important thing, in my mind, is that thankfulness is fundamentally natural, and, grateful people make gratefulness contagious. Isn't it a happy thought that every one of us can find that "crisp, electric spark of joy" in each day throughout the year?

With Muir in mind, I remember stopping along a mountain pass in Scotland once to enjoy the gorgeous view. I was so full of gratefulness for my ancestral homeland, and smiled to read the highway sign. The name of the pass was "Rest and Be Thankful." May that be our trail to thankfulness at every season.

Winter reflections, Beaverdam, Asheville NC

Four
Adopting the Bethlehem Baby

As someone born and adopted on Christmas Day, it was no surprise to some in my family that I chose to attend a Christian college and then enter seminary to become an ordained minister. For me, December has always been a time to reflect on both the shining star of a loving family and the severed trunks of beautiful trees cut down to "celebrate life." Ironies abound when it comes to the holidays, particularly when a person no longer believes the literal truth of the stories but appreciates the "spirit of giving" and symbols of peace and good will.

A Buddhist priest and a Christian minister went into a brewery … no, seriously, they once sat with a mixed group of church and sangha folks to teach a course on the book, *Living Buddha, Living Christ* by Thich Nhat Hanh. The priest was my friend Lee, and I was the minister. We met in the church where I was parish associate and then we gathered at the Zen farm where Lee had practiced for many years. Lee and I were already friends and colleagues, since he served as the chair of the street chaplaincy where I was interfaith chaplain. I also had enjoyed several personal retreats at the farm with its deep green fields rolling down toward the blue Pacific. A beautiful place where anyone, of any faith or no faith, can feel welcome.

Every student in that course was moved by the respectful manner in which the book treats Jesus as a kind of brother to Buddha, and each person could see how easy it is for two leaders of two historic faiths to sit together, teach together and work alongside each other as friends.

Later that year, Lee and I invited faith leaders from churches, synagogues, mosques, meetings and more to celebrate Thanksgiving together. That was in 1997, and that interfaith service still happens every year on the night before Thanksgiving. What always made those celebrations so wonderful was the diversity of the assembly, grateful and giving. Yet what made it very special was including people who lived outside—those who often feel excluded from our communities. Not only were unhoused neighbors invited to attend—they were an important part of the service, no more and no less important than clergy, as they joined in by leading music, reading, and telling their stories of living without homes.

Before sharing a common supper, a procession flowed forward carrying blankets, gloves, coats, sleeping bags, and other essentials. This was a very emotional moment—we all could see how simple gifts were helping people survive. No one with a safe dwelling place walked out into the cold that night without a deep gratitude for a place to call home, and a deeper concern for their neighbors sleeping outside with nothing but stars for a roof.

One pastor spoke at this Thanksgiving Eve service and said that anyone who was treating home-challenged human beings with compassion was "doing the work of Jesus." All the assembled folk, of all faiths and no faiths, were nodding their heads. Even non-Christians understand what that means. An ancient Palestinian rabbi taught people to show love and compassion and to work for justice. It's a message echoed in Buddha and

Krishna, Confucius and Muhammad ("in the name of The One, the compassionate and merciful"). What could be more inclusive than that? What an energizing call to live and learn together!

I was born on Christmas Day. Born and adopted on Christmas. Maybe Jesus would have understood that feeling since, in the original story, he was "adopted" by Joseph. Then he was "'adopted" by a ragged group of outsiders, and later "adopted" again by a powerful institution called by his name. Unfortunately, at times Jesus's adopted family seems more distracted by "believing in the baby" than devoted to living his grown-up message.

Do you ever wonder who "owns" Jesus? That's a troubling question for some, but it might be good to ask from time to time. Is there one church that can claim he belongs to them, where they and they alone know who Jesus is and what he wants? I grew up in a church that believed that. The belief, or sentiment, was unspoken, but it was in the very air we breathed; it was certainly the feeling I got.

That seems a rather sad thing to do to the baby in the manger or the man on the mountainside. Could anyone own him?

Lee would always have a peaceful smile on his face when Jesus was the topic of discussion. He was happy to be sitting in a meeting even when people were trying to "preach the gospel" or say prayers "in Jesus's name." That didn't bother my Buddhist friend. But it bothered me. I didn't like the disrespect shown to Lee, or other people of different faiths, or the group of street folk sitting as captive audience for someone's "mission."

For many years, even as a minister, I was displeased and disappointed to hear people evangelize "the poor." I wondered if these same people would try to convert Mary, Joseph, and the Baby himself. Because, as we all know, they weren't "insiders" either.

In this season of light, maybe it would be good for us to adopt some enlightened ways of thinking. If we can adopt more compassion and understanding, maybe more than one baby would smile.

Five
The Good beyond Us and Them

I think it's good to shine a light on the positive things that communities do to inspire, such as this service that made some effort at including a chorus of voices from many traditions. While no specifically non-theistic voices (Ethical Humanists, Freethinkers) were invited, a number of avowedly secular groups did participate. I think the message was still something freethinkers could sign on to: enlightened good works in the community.

One winter evening my wife Carol and I enjoyed the "Let it Shine" event at the Unitarian Universalist Congregation of Asheville, where hundreds of people came together for a "celebration of community light." Though many express fears and frustrations over our nation's leadership choices, there is hope in the air in the season of light.

I'm used to participating in these welcoming events, so it was impressive to see representatives of many groups coming forward to simply light a candle and place it in sand. Flames were glowing to honor a large number of agencies and congregations including the Asheville City Schools Foundation, the multi-racial engagement nonprofit Building Bridges, the Center for Diversity Education (housed at UNC Asheville), local branches of the YMCA, ACLU, and NAACP, Congregation Beth Israel, the Episcopal Cathedral of All Souls, and many others. We felt surrounded by good people doing good work on behalf of everyone.

Long-time civil rights attorney Frank Goldsmith, representing Carolina Jews for Justice, read a powerful community statement of solidarity that included these encouraging lines: "We are truly blessed to live in a community that today strives to welcome and support people of every creed, ethnicity, religion, background, gender and orientation.... There are so many organizations and individuals in Asheville that work every day to reach out across barriers, bringing greater understanding into our community.... When we look at all of these efforts together, it is easy to see that there is a strong web of resources and profound hope for our shared future."

Far from idealistic, this statement set the tone for speakers from Green Opportunities, a job-training organization dedicated to helping former inmates return to productive lives and jobs; the Asheville Jewish Community Center; the Hispanic community organization Nuestro Centro; the Literacy Council of Buncombe County; and Tranzmission, a local program offering support and advocacy for transsexual and transitioning individuals. A Buncombe County Commissioner, Ellen Frost, spoke passionately about the need for strong coalitions and firm actions against hatred and exclusion. She received a standing ovation for the commission's commitment to justice. African American, Latina, Libyan, and English speakers stirred the shoulder-to-shoulder audience with poems in various colorful languages.

This is the kind of thing that can happen when agencies, congregations, and civil leaders decide to communicate, cooperate, and collaborate. I think it's pretty close to what people mean when they speak of a "healthy community."

As a secular person, I was delighted to see that this event, facilitated by religious folks and held in a religious venue, was not focused on faith but the concerns and issues we all care about regardless of belief systems. The operative "belief" is believing in the power of reasonable people to agree on commonalities—what unites rather than divides us.

The statement ended with this energizing invitation:

"Today, we are calling upon this entire community to join us in making a choice to shine a light of love in the world; to reject hatred and to seek out ways to quench our own biases with curiosity about those who seem different."

Who would not answer that call?

Events and celebrations like this are certainly not merely hand-clapping or hand-wringing times for liberals and progressives. I kept looking around wondering if there were conservatives and Republicans in the crowd. I'd like to think so. And maybe they would be a bit uncomfortable listening to some of the rhetoric. Yet I think it was clear that though most voices were clearly on the left end of the political spectrum, the overall theme of "community light" was not excluding "those and them" at all.

And here's one funny thing: I looked around and thought of seculars too, aware that many of us might feel just the way some conservatives might feel sitting in that crowd. This is the lesson some never learn: to consider the feelings of others; to ask who is being excluded by our words or actions; to look beyond our own voice to the voices who may be missing.

At one point of the program, two Latinas were reading a poem — first in Spanish, then in English. It seemed very long and my attention was slipping, hoping the poem would be over soon. But I had to focus and appreciate the powerful words, realizing these were words from people rarely heard, listened to, or valued. When a gentleman rose to read a poem in Arabic I had the same feeling; from the response, it appeared the gathering greatly valued this voice, too.

After her many travels around the world, Eleanor Roosevelt once reflected, "I cannot understand or believe that anything that has to be preserved by fear will stand permanently against a system which offers love and trust among peoples and removes fear so that all feel free to think and express their ideas" (*Autobiography*, 1961).

Eleanor seemed to understand that fear diminishes when we get to know people who are different, and celebrate the good beyond Us and Them. I saw the seeds of this growing right here in Asheville.

Six
When a Minister No Longer Believes

When writing for a newspaper, it seems important to introduce readers to resources and options they may not be aware of. One way I do this is to weave in aspects of my own story that may help some people understand non-religious choices. This column explains stepping stones in the path from a life in the church to a life after faith, highlighting the honesty and courage evident in The Clergy Project (theclergyproject.org).

Those of us who grew up in the church, who went to Sunday School, youth groups, Bible studies, mission trips, and prayer meetings, know that Christian faith can become your whole life. There is deep satisfaction knowing that the "church family" is your community and God is your companion.

Some of us are "called into the ministry," choosing to serve the church and the world as ordained clergy. We go to seminary to study Hebrew, Greek, Biblical Theology, Religious History, Church Government, Sacraments, Preaching, and much more. If we complete three to four years of course work and pass ordination exams, we may be awarded a Master of Divinity degree and sent off to find a pastorate wherever that "call" leads.

Along this vocational path (vocation derives from the Latin word "to call"), some discover that working in a congregation is not where they feel they need to be.

They have skills for teaching or counseling, or directing a nonprofit. Their "congregation" is not in a church building but in an agency, a school, prison, hospital or hospice, a university, the military, or on the street. These untidy, secular congregations are wonderfully uncomfortable settings where a chaplain may be more appropriate than a minister. Since chaplains are out among people of many faiths as well as atheists, agnostics, and freethinkers, their "mission" can transform into something very different from what church and seminary taught.

Chaplains tend to be out on the "edges" where faith issues are not so clear; they have many things in common with pastors (priests and rabbis, too) who serve more traditional congregations yet find their faith is morphing into something very different than what faith or ministry has always looked like. Some discover over time that they no longer believe what they are "supposed" to believe. Maybe they question some passages in the Bible, or some church teaching just doesn't make sense any longer. Maybe they aren't sure any more if the dogmas, prayers, or sacraments hold the same meaning for them or for their world. (Needless to say, congregational clergy can share these same questions.)

Even back in seminary, many of us had big questions about theology and the church. We were constantly grappling with god-issues. In fact, many of our professors encouraged this vigorous engagement with theological concerns. Those who avoid hard, honest thinking out of fear they may doubt their cherished beliefs might judge these professors for urging this intense wrestling with ideas, but most of us found it energizing. We sensed that many people in the pews, as well as many outside the church, were troubled by similar doubts and questions. Parishioners as well as pastors themselves may feel there is no one who understands their inner conflicts.

This can lead to a critical, disruptive stage of faith that can shake a person to the core. When your whole life, your identity, your vocation, everything has centered around God, faith, and congregation, what do you do when it all begins to evaporate?

In 2011, a small group of ministers and academics shared their loss of faith with each other. They knew that there were other clergy in ministries across the country who carried a heart-wrenching secret: they did not believe anymore. Where would they find support?

The Clergy Project (TCP) was formed with a mission "to provide support, community, and hope to current and former religious professionals who no longer believe in the supernatural." I joined in 2012; there are now nearly 800 members in the online community.

Is a pastor who doesn't believe everything in the Bible or church teachings being dishonest? From my experience with TCP, it is clear that many who still serve congregations struggle with this ethical tension. They are professionals, trained to be truthful and live a life of integrity. Not only do they love serving others, their livelihoods (including pensions) depend on the ministry. Can you imagine the painful dilemma they feel in this impossible situation? Some risk losing significant relationships by "coming out" as nonbelievers.

To my way of thinking, no one "loses" their faith—they choose to let it go; they make a rational decision to move on from believing to not believing. This can be very gradual over years, or happen more suddenly, for instance when one rejects the doctrine of hell, atonement, or the virgin birth. An unraveling occurs and they have to admit their faith has no grounding.

There are many good people who are trained counselors, teachers, and speakers but for whom the church is no longer their home or family. If we have compassion and curiosity, maybe they can show us how to have the courage to be more honest and truthful.

Seven
Holy Books

One of the most controversial subjects a writer on religion must call attention to is the variety of scriptures offered by world faiths. My years as a chaplain form an endless storehouse of memories for me. Since I spent many years providing "spiritual literature" to people as well as teaching groups about "sacred scriptures," I now wonder what that meant and what it accomplished. Without regret, I feel some satisfaction that I have introduced countless people to alternative viewpoints beginning with the "inspired" literature of history.

When I was a jail chaplain one of the most satisfying parts of my work was bringing books inside to prisoners. These were mostly "spiritual" or "inspirational" books like *Daily Word, Each Day a New Beginning* (AA meditations), or selections from "wisdom teachers." What surprised inmates the most was how happy I was to bring them scriptures. I handed out hundreds of free Bibles, but I also honored requests for other holy books as well as pagan, Wiccan, and other literature which incarcerated people have a constitutional right to access.

Many people think there is only one "true" scripture, which is a nice idea—but one that doesn't hold water in the real world. Jews have their Torah; Christians have their Bible; Muslims their Qur'an; Hindus their Gita; Buddhists their Sutras; Sikhs their Granth Sahib; and of course there are Mormon books and Christian Science books and many, many others. There is a world of scripture for a world of religions.

What makes one book exceptionally special for some is the belief that it was "given," "handed down," "delivered" or even dictated by a god or gods. And this makes those who "received a revelation" very exceptionally special too. Unfortunately, many forget or choose to ignore the fact that they and their cherished book are but one patch stitched into the massive quilt of belief.

Let's talk about one book, the only sacred scripture most Americans ever read: the Bible. The word "bible" simply comes from the Greek word *byblos*, meaning "book." Some say—and I don't doubt—this one book is the most published on the planet: Gideons has distributed over 2 billion copies. The Qur'an is a close second, and there are millions of copies of the Hindu Vedas and Bhagavad Gita ("Song of the Lord") as well.

People say "old" and "new" testaments, but after thousands of years I think we can say it's all pretty old. Old doesn't mean it isn't worthwhile to read, that there aren't some stories worth retelling in those ancient pages. But, as Emerson asked, why shouldn't we, too, have an "original relation" to the universe, nature, god? Why should we always look over our shoulder and listen to voices from long ago? Isn't there a "God's Word" spoken today? If so, how would we know?

Holy books raise a whole library full of questions!

Once, in a gathering of inmates, I asked the question, "What does the Bible say?" This caused puzzled looks all around. After a number of comments and guesses, I joked that "The Bible doesn't say anything; it's a book. People say what they think it says." Some groans. Some heads nodding. It wasn't really a joke, of course. The truth was sinking in: a book does not speak. If we rely on "authorities" to tell us what the book says and what it means, we are relying on them to tell us what a divine voice says. As long as we keep that in mind, we'll be fine. Maybe. It might be more important to read it for ourselves and think about it. We might decide we don't believe some of the things written thousands of years ago. Who says that's a bad thing?

We've all heard of people who have died for a book. And, sadly, we hear of people who kill for a book. Books that are supposed to be sacred sources of peace and compassion and justice. Strange how we handle them — use, and misuse them.

Naturalist John Burroughs wrote of "Nature's great book" and said it is important "to see with your reason as well as with your perceptions, that is to be an observer and to read the book of nature aright" ("Reading the Book of Nature," in *Ways of Nature*, 1905). It's hard to be a good observer of the world around us if we have our noses in dusty old books that speak of other worlds; if our spiritual life is rooted in the past, tied only to books and ideas of long ago, we won't hear what we need to hear today.

The best option may simply be to read, think, reflect and read more, even as we observe more, learning from the life surrounding us.

A French Jesuit, Jean-Pierre deCaussade, was a mystic in these matters. He wrote encouragement to some nuns, and his writings were published under the heretical title *The Sacrament of the Present Moment*. He essentially said, "living scriptures are being written today." Remarkable words. Wisdom texts are being written now — maybe you and I are writing them?

Maybe, when it comes right down to it, believer or not, life is our Bible, and it's open for us to read, and to write.

Bridge in shadows, UNC Asheville Botanical Gardens

Eight
Ever Mindful of the Needs

Many of us who identify as atheist, agnostic, or freethinker have meaningful family stories of how and why we emerged. Yet many of us also carry great admiration and respect for the examples set by our parents or others dear to us. While some have had awful and even abusive experiences in their upbringing, for others there is no intention to mock or scoff at the way our loved ones practiced their faith. In fact, sometimes the lessons we pack out when we leave faith continue to hold throughout our lives. In this column, a personal family story leads into a reflection on thoughtfulness and compassion.

Growing up in the Pacific Northwest, just north of Seattle, Washington, my sister and I ate dinner with our parents almost every night. When Dad wasn't working swing shift at Boeing, he would do a little baking, Mom would cook up meat-and-potato dishes, and we would all sit down to eat together. Does this sound like an old movie?

Dad was a devout man who loved to laugh and make others laugh—or groan—at his puns and silly jokes. But when we sat down at the family table, all heads would bow for Dad's grace. I don't recall that he ever said more than these simple words: "Thank you, Lord, for these thy gifts which we are about to receive; and let us be ever mindful of the needs of others; Amen." Those words, especially the last phrase, stuck in my mind as my mother's pot roast stuck to my ribs.

"Let us be ever mindful of the needs of others." An early experience at a downtown rescue mission drove the words home. Our youth group was serving meals to a large room full of people on skid row. ("Skid row" or "skid road" originated in Seattle and referred to the way lumber mills would skid logs down the hills into the Puget Sound—the inhabitants of that area were the "skid road" people.) We scurried around the dim-lit lunchroom bringing heaping plates of hot food to each table. Calling out to each other, we made sure everyone had a plate. Several times, my friends called over to me, "Chris, we need a plate over here" and once, when I was making my way back to the kitchen, a voice came out of a dark corner, "Thank you, Chris!" In my shyness I probably just waved and hurried on, but the words haunted me. This person, a nameless, faceless Someone, heard my name and used it to thank me personally for the simple act of running plates of food to tables.

I never forgot that gesture, and never forgot that the smallest action can hold great meaning, for the giver and the receiver. As I went on to study biblical theology and world religions in college, then to seminary to study ministry, I carried that "Thank you, Chris" with me. I was drawn to do what I could do for people, whether they thanked me or not, and chaplaincy was a perfect way to practice basic helping.

Listening to another person; offering the human touch of a hug or a smile; buying a sandwich for a stranger; giving a ride or a blanket. All are examples of doing something that becomes natural after a while, when you're being thoughtful. No more saving the world. No more rescuing someone from addiction or damnation.

Those of us who do this kind of work, where theology and beliefs don't really matter much any longer, find a contentment in simply "being present" for another human being to do what can be done in the moment, and that is usually the best that can be done.

"Stan" came in off the street one afternoon, sat down, introduced himself and said, "I have a message for you." With a smile, I swiveled in my chair and said, with a bit of skepticism, "Oh, okaaay." Stan instructed me, and my assistant, to hold out a hand, palm up. He said, "Now, put all the bad stuff you've done into your hand." Smiles got wider. "ALL of them," he insisted. We concentrated. "Now, squeeze your hand closed." We did. "Put some more in there and squeeze again, there's more room!" With a laugh, we followed obediently. "Is that all?" Stan asked, looking at us intently. Satisfied we were being honest, he said, "Now, give it to me." He opened his hands and went to each of us to dump our heavy hands into his. Immediately he stood, shook his hands toward the floor, and said, "It's gone! Congratulations!" He sat back down with a big grin. We were amused but expressed appreciation and then offered him a cup of coffee.

Ever mindful. Stan's little ritual somehow helped, especially out among some very broken and wounded people. Maybe like a new sacrament.

The needs of others. Could it be so simple, to invite someone to give away their pain, their grief, their loneliness, their self-hatred, if only for a minute? Is this why some religious teachings have such a hold on people? If we were more mindful, could each of us lift some weight off another?

I suspect there is more odd, needful wisdom for us on the skid roads and in the dark corners that expose our own needs as well.

Nine
Give Fire to the Dreams

This is another secular devotional — a meditation on a meditation. I like to draw in thoughts and ideas from various sources to consider and contemplate. Galeano's compact book of thoughts offers some fruitful sparks to kindle the fire of imagination — something both faithful and freethinkers can enjoy.

I was honored when a friend gave me a wonderful book by Latin American author Eduardo Galeano. It's titled *Children of the Days: A Calendar of Human History*. You know those books that have an inspirational reading for every day of the year? Well, this is one, but it's not. Galeano is a humanist freethinker whose delightful collection of daily wisdom ranges from historical events in politics and religion to inventions, celebrations, and strange events. You can find yourself smiling or even laughing, just before you are shaken to your senses.

The May 15 selection has a title I would call a "brainsticker" (like a bumpersticker for the mind): "May Tomorrow Be More Than Just Another Name for Today." We hear from homeless, jobless youth in Spain marching through the streets in 2011: their call for justice reverberated around the world. As Galeano says, "the voices of the 'indignant' crossed the borders drawn on maps."

What was their message?

"Turn off the TV and turn on the street."

"Not too little money, too many crooks."

"Markets rule, I didn't vote for them."

"They decide for us without us."

"I'm looking for my rights. Anyone seen them?"

And then these marginalized youth in Spain shout out something that all people of conscience in any land will find stunning: "If they won't let us dream, we won't let them sleep."

Powerful, energizing words. A call to secular and spiritual people—all people—to wake up and take positive action.

Children of The Days reminds us we have so much more to learn, and much of that learning is remembering—recalling our own history and the countless histories of other people in other nations and times. It should give us a good dose of hope to build our knowledge through consistent, even insistent, education. Insistent like those young Spanish marchers—indignant but not ignorant. We wake up to realize we are each a child of the days, history is ours to make, and we can contribute something to each day, to each life we touch.

Recently I went to a colleague's home where she had gathered counselors, religious leaders, teachers, organizers, writers, and artists. Over dinner we had conversations in which many of us shared our questions and concerns for the coming year with its disturbing uncertainties. Our host ended the evening with a circle of candles. We each held one flame and every face was lit up. We were invited to look around and name what we celebrate, what we grieve, what we hope for. Simple. This could have been a church choir, a pagan circle, a meditation group. It might have been in a synagogue, a mosque, a temple, or an open field. It may have been simple, but the ritual flickered with meaning.

For his December 31 selection, Galeano tells of an ancient Roman cure: hang the word "Abracadabra" around your neck. He says the word meant, "Give your fire until the last of your days." Giving our fire is another way of talking about dreams, whether we live in the blue ridges of the hills, warm and safe, or in the cold corners of a downtown alleyway. What is it that kindles our humanity?

Music is one fire we can stoke. "We are made of music," says Galeano. We may have no idea what that means, but music easily crosses borders, and perhaps we'll discover neighbors who can teach us new songs, maybe people who are very different, who believe very differently, who have different politics, religions, races, nationalities.

And what if we imagined the unimaginable? What if this was a circle of Republicans and Democrats? Is that so crazy? What if a candle was held by a child in Aleppo, in Mosul, in Moscow, in South Sudan and East Los Angeles? What word would we hang around our necks? Abracadabra … give your fire!

What lights my candle through darker seasons is to be aware of what nature is doing, and pay attention. Many of our wild neighbors are hibernating now, sleeping—maybe dreaming—and rejuvenating even below the surface. Just under the roots and rocks, just beyond our view, wild things are resting, recharging for what's ahead. If we can learn from them—from the hidden things around us—and take our cues from the cycle of seasons, we may be more prepared for the fire, the music and the dreams that make our lives worth living.

It might just be true that we won't sleep very well until we assist more people in our world to dream. Our common dream is that tomorrow will not just be another name for yesterday, or today.

How will you give your fire day by day, year by year?

Ten
Secular Prayers

Prayer is fundamental to any practice of faith. Yet, for some of us, prayer also raises a host of questions often quite uncomfortable for believers to consider. What is prayer? What do people intend when they are praying? Is there a way to define and practice prayer for nonbelievers? What do you do when prayers are not "answered"? Then we might ask if a secular person can "pray" in some way. If so, what would that look like?

Most of us are taught that prayer is "talking with God." That is one definition, but it doesn't cover all the ways human beings try to connect with something greater than themselves. As a chaplain I was often asked to pray for someone. I was happy to stop whatever I was doing and sit with the person, to ask what was troubling them. More often than not, the person would forget their request for me to pray with them. They really wanted someone to pay attention to their concerns and to hear them. This is much easier and perhaps more meaningful when you can actually see the person you are speaking with.

Of course, Christians aren't the only people who pray. Jews, Muslims, Sufis, Hindus, Buddhists, and many others have practices of prayer. Some see prayer as primarily contemplative—reflective and quiet; some like to chant, sing or dance; some meditate, breathing silently while sitting or walking. And silence itself is, for some people, a form of prayer.

Generally speaking, prayer could be understood

as a practice of attentiveness, or as Buddhists say, mindfulness. Gautama from India was called "The Buddha" because he had found a way to "wake up" through peaceful meditation. Waking up and paying attention to our surroundings and our lives seems simple, but it can be difficult. Yet, understood in this way, almost everyone prays (or meditates) in one way or another.

As an interfaith chaplain I was privileged to be with people who were praying in synagogues, mosques, temples, and other traditional sanctuaries. Some of us organized multi-faith prayer gatherings where many religions including Native American, Bahá'í, Mormon, Wiccan, and even evangelical folks shared their prayers. I say "even" evangelicals because I was sometimes told "we can't pray with non-Christians." As a former evangelical myself, I understood what they were saying and why they were saying that—it was just so disappointing.

When you pray with others who pray differently than you, it can be a wake-up all by itself! And what's to be afraid of when we learn from new experiences?

But what about non-religious people? Can a person pray who does not believe in a God or the supernatural? Once again, it depends on who defines prayer. If a practice of mindful awareness—being awake and attentive to the present moment of living—is "prayer," then of course a nonbeliever can pray. Yet I don't know anyone who is an atheist or agnostic or freethinker who "prays," as such. Prayer has been strictly defined by religious authorities and doctrine for many centuries. It has too much baggage for many who were raised with prayer and no longer view it the "orthodox" way.

Ralph Waldo Emerson's famous line puts another spin

on this: "Prayer is the contemplation of the facts of life from the highest point of view" (*Self-Reliance*, 1840). I'm not being flippant or disrespectful to say there are times I take this quite literally. When I climb a tree or ascend a trail to a mountaintop, I can't help but contemplate the facts of life. To get to those "higher places" for new perspective, to fill the lungs with mountain air and fill the senses with life's beauty and wonder, is prayer enough for me.

Some may be shocked to hear there is such a thing as "secular prayer." I completely understand. In my youthful days, people said I was so good at prayer they wanted to pray like me. I was so proud of my humility! And it truly felt as though the Lord of the Universe was my Friend and Brother—I talked to Him constantly. With more life experience, a "higher point of view" brought me down to earth. It became clear that when we stop looking to other worlds for help, we learn to accept that this world is good all by itself—it's all we have. We may find that "real prayer" is giving a word of encouragement, showing kindness or working for justice.

It may be uncomfortable to hear that much of what we call prayer is actually talking to ourselves, wishing someone—Someone—would pay attention to us and do our bidding.

In his first book, *Nature* (1836), Emerson offers a delightful way for spiritual and secular people to "pray" together: "To the attentive eye, each moment of the year has its own beauty, and in the same field, it beholds, every hour, a picture which was never seen before, and which shall never be seen again."

If this is prayer at its best—at its most awake, aware and alive—then, by all means, "Let us pray"!

Old cabin chimney, Nantahala National Forest

Eleven
One Nature Indivisible

We may pledge to be an undivided nation, but how's that working? What if we borrowed the famous patriotic phrase and referred to something larger, like nature? There may be some common "unifiers" to draw us together across all boundaries and divisiveness. When we hear or see or experience something that shows how un-divided we can be, we are presented with profound images that can guide our actions and even our beliefs.

In early January, 2017, Carol and I were cozied down in a cabin in the Nantahala forest for three nights. After two days snowed in at our place in Asheville, the rain on the cabin roof was a warming welcome.

I'd like to say we read books when we came back from explorations near the lake or rivers—and we did read—but the lamps weren't very good for light, so we watched some shows on the flatscreen (I have to say I prefer a cabin without a screen). We happened to be there to watch President Obama's final address in Chicago, feeling some sadness to see him leave after the eight years we knew him as president. For balance, the next morning we watched Mr. Trump's first news conference. We had a very different response to that, but this column is not about partisan politics. Well, it is, but I'll come back to that.

Hiking up a leg of the Appalachian Trail, we found ourselves in the burned area of Tellico Gap, where forest fires had ravaged the mountains a few months before. The smell of the autumn fires was strong yet the trail was still in good condition. We were thankful for firefighters each step up the root-laced path. I was reflecting on the impressive way men and women from all over the country came to WNC to fight those fires. On those steep and slippery slopes it isn't hard to imagine the incredibly difficult and dangerous work those crews struggled with in the battle against exploding trees and hot flames whipped up by unpredictable winds. Charred stumps and scarred remnants of rhododendrons, mountain laurel and larger trees surrounded our ascent. When we reached the ridge and the fire tower we were intending to climb, the fog was so thick we couldn't see anything. As a light rain began to fall, we turned back and enjoyed a slow saunter winding down in the mist.

The morning we left the cabin we drove over another gap. Due to the fires and recent snow, another trail was closed, so we continued down the twisting road toward Franklin. Rounding a corner, we saw a white car angled into a ditch. A lady frantically waved us down so we pulled over to help. We put on our coats and crossed the road to see how she had wedged her car into the slope, one front tire spinning. We did our best to push and rock the car—but it was no use.

About this time a bearded guy in a large truck came down the mountain. We waved him over and without hesitation he pulled over to see what he could do. We all got branches and rocks for traction, but it still wasn't enough. Then, two young forest rangers stopped to help. Finally, another man with a truck and trailer joined us.

Everyone looked over the situation. The Latina driver was nervously joking with us, concerned that we might damage her rental car. The first guy got a tow rope and climbed under to attach it, making a comment to us, "If anything goes wrong, my name is Barack Obama—he's on his way out—so you can blame me." We chuckled.

The car was carefully pulled down one side of the ditch, enough so the woman ranger could drive it out with ease. The lady was so happy, thanking each of us with a handshake and smile.

Six strangers helping one stranded woman in need. No question; no hesitation. We all just stopped and assisted. Were we Republicans or Democrats? Liberals or conservatives? Were we rich or poor, employed or unemployed? Were we Christians or Muslims or Atheists? North Carolinians or from another state? In the moment, no one cared about that. Someone needed help, and we helped … like the firefighters from across the nation. What does it matter what their politics or religion or bank account may tell us about them? Strangers don't seem so strange when we realize that we are strangers to them too—and it doesn't have to make any difference.

Something we call "America." We live here together. It's our country, our nation, our land—not "those people" and "our people." But it's too easy to get stuck in a ditch and forget, too easy to think we are the true Americans and this is our nation, not "theirs."

I reflect back to that burned-over trail in Nantahala. We stumbled over blackened roots for miles and got soot on our boots. Even in the midst of so much destruction, the forest was already regenerating itself, and us. Tripping over those intertwined roots was a step-by-step reminder that the land — nature itself — marks us by rain and fire, mind and muscle ... we are indivisible.

Twelve
I Can't Wait to See Heaven

When someone asks me how I came to believe and then came to disbelieve I have a story to tell: the short version and the long one. What may be surprising to some is the appreciation I still have for those years when I sincerely believed God lived within me, guided me, and spoke to me. I admit that it pained me when the "brothers and sisters in Christ" who were so dear to me disappeared during college, many of them never to be heard of again. Now, in the Google age, it would be easy for any of them to find me, but they might not like what I've become. We grew up, and maybe grew out of faith. I know I did. But I've never lost the memory of how it felt to be so self-assured, accepted and loved by "friends in faith" as we awaited our joyful meeting with Jesus in the air on our way home.

How many of us enjoyed church youth groups when we were growing up? If you're like me, you spent many hours with other youth in Sunday classes, chapels, camps, concerts, and conferences. A very formative time.

We did a lot of singing. Apart from rejoicing in the fellowship of friends and apart from praying and reading the Bible together, singing was the highlight of our gatherings. I learned to strum the guitar in our Presbyterian group, then went on to sing in the church choir and a youth chorus performing in services around town. In college, I sang in our chapel choir. Don't tell anyone, but I even sang at a Billy Graham crusade in a Seattle stadium. I don't think anyone noticed me, though: there were 8,000 voices.

At that young age, my brain was saturated with many of those songs. As a result, I still remember a lot of the words and even some of the feelings I had while singing them with my friends. We sang:

"I've got a home in gloryland that outshines the sun."

"Mama taught me how to pray before I reached the age of seven;
And when I'm down on my knees that's when I'm close to heaven."

"When the shadows appear, And the night draws near, And the day is past and gone,
At the river I stand. Guide my feet, hold my hand; Take my hand, precious Lord, lead me home."

"I can't wait to see heaven, and to walk on the streets of pure gold;
I can't wait to check into my mansion, and get my sleeping bag unrolled."

"Heaven is a wonderful place, filled with glory and grace;
I wanna see my Savior's face, heaven is a wonderful place."

From 9th grade to college, we sang these songs. Hundreds of youthful voices singing praises and prayers, joyful and tearful, full of emotion.

Then, the countless hymns, gospel songs, and folk ballads that stir a higher vision, like "Be Thou My Vision": "High King of Heaven, my victory won; May I reach Heaven's joys, O bright Heaven's Sun! Heart of my own heart, whatever befall; Still be my Vision, O Ruler of all."

Notice any pattern here? Any common thread?

We were only teens, but we didn't feel at home; we were ready to go, ready to be taken away, up there, up to heaven. We would have done anything to get there. If our young lives were over, fantastic: Someone who loved us was calling us Home.

This was the 1970s, and *The Late, Great Planet Earth* was a bestseller. We were ecstatic to be among the "Jesus People"; our favorite films were *Godspell* and *Jesus Christ, Superstar*. We fully expected to witness the Second Coming of Christ and be "caught up in glory with Jesus" when he returned — very soon! — to "take us home."

Even now, looking back, I can feel the love we felt for each other, for God, and the deep longing to go home to be with God. Very strong; very compelling. And now, sad and a little bit frightening.

In the 1800s the great naturalist John Muir ventured into the "cathedrals" and "temples" of the high Sierra Nevada range and walked straight into paradise. Muir was raised in a strict religious family but found a new, natural religion in the wilderness. He wrote:

"Some of the days I have spent alone in the depths of the wilderness have shown me that immortal life beyond the grave is not essential to perfect happiness" (*Journals*).

"The forests ... seem kindly familiar, and the lakes and meadows and glad singing streams. I should like to dwell with them forever.... A new heaven and a new earth every day" (*My First Summer in the Sierras*).

Describing his mountain temple in the same book, Muir listens to the birds and breezes — "the sweetest church music I ever enjoyed."

That's the heaven I look for now.

Why didn't I hear about John Muir when I was a young man? I loved nature, but there were so many voices insisting that I "look higher" than this "fallen world." Why were so many preachers and evangelists pointing me to "heaven's shores" and "my home up yonder"? How could adults—who should have known better—encourage my friends and me to spend our precious adolescence singing praises to a God who was always "calling us home"? It's a wonder we didn't all drink Koolaid or jump off a bridge.

There were some spiritual songs that kept our feet on the earth. "Peace Like a River," "Make Me an Instrument," "Stand By Me," and others.

I wonder, if more people of faith joined in song with secular voices, maybe the world would hear something quite heavenly.

Cataloochee streaming, Smoky Mountains

Thirteen
Other Rivers

I often circle back to a grounded naturalism that appreciates the common beauty of the land. At times, I sense I'm slipping into an almost meditative presentation. For people who live near parks and pathways or those who feel disconnected from nature, it seems good to remind them, and all of us, of the simple (secular) lessons that can be found along whatever rivers or streams we encounter and explore.

Our first exploration of February took us out of town, off the highways into the hills and hollers. Winding up the mountains we were a little stunned by the poverty tucked back in the woods, not far from the mansions and money of the city. Who are the people of the "sticks" and what are their stories? The images stick with you, disturbing, intriguing. We drove on until the pavement became a bumpy gravel road over and down into the national park. Elk outnumbered the iPhone crowd and we arrived at the trailhead in Cataloochee.

Hitching up the hiking shoes, we followed a main branch of the stream a few miles, crossed some bridges and never saw a soul. The chilly winter's night left notes for us along the way—icicles on branches and moss, icy patches by the cold waters. As we snapped a few photos in an attempt to capture beauty that cannot be captured, the forest absorbed our attention and soaked us in.

I was so captivated by one icy fall cascading over

slick green boulders that I completely missed another branch of the river washing into the flow a stone's throw away. So focused was I on focusing the camera on the up-close artistry of nature, I neglected to look just a little out of my field of vision to see the greater picture. My wife pointed out small rivulets snaking down under tree roots and leafy bushes.

Nature's simple lessons are usually basic and rather obvious—if we're paying attention. Yet, the instructors and textbooks in the natural classrooms can be as perplexing and complex as the human brain (I often think of the brain as a pulsing landscape of living streams churning with blood and ideas).

What is the "Greatest River on the Planet"? The Nile (the longest), the Amazon (largest amount of water), the Congo (deepest)? Growing up in Washington, I thought the greatest river was the mighty Columbia. But my favorite rivers had Native American names like Skykomish, Stillaguamish, and Skagit. The best ones had lots of fish and were so clear, bubbling from the Cascade or Olympic mountains, you could drink from them. It didn't take too many years to realize that the greatest river was whichever one I was standing by or hiking near or skinny-dipping in. More honestly, maybe the greatest one is yet to be found.

It seems that when we step back a little, we see something "greater" and "better" than what we see in a narrow, restricted view. I enjoy observing the world close-up, to find something delightful right at my feet. But it constantly amazes me to stand or climb higher, to take in the larger, deeper, wider perspective.

Here's a real-time example from the current turbulence

of political streams. Many people want to change a law—the Johnson Amendment—to allow religious congregations to support, endorse, and campaign for candidates. Some feel that the government has not allowed free speech for people of faith, although no one has been prosecuted under this amendment since it was adopted in the 1950s, and those who participate in "Pulpit Freedom Sunday" are not bothered by the IRS. These folks think that if their pastor could proclaim one candidate as "God's chosen" (as some did in the last election), there would once again be true religious freedom in America.

Rather than debate this here, I want to step back, stand up straight and imagine what the land would look like if Lyndon Johnson's law was "destroyed." Let's say every church, synagogue, mosque, and temple were suddenly free to be as partisan as they wish. Joyous congregations would gather every Sunday, especially during election season, in celebration of this or that politician. Think of it. All of their tax-free monies could flow into the great Republican river or Democratic stream.

As we know, these houses of worship are nonprofit organizations untaxed by the government, which means all Americans—all of us, religious or not—give religious groups a break and congregations can raise millions to give to anyone they choose.

Now, step up a little higher on this boulder in the stream of imagination. Local churches (and other "houses of God") could finally be free to identify as First Church of the Redeemer's Republicans or First Church of the Democratic Christ. Then churches could begin to paint their sanctuaries either red or blue, making it convenient for townsfolk or tourists to immediately see from a distance which political persuasion is praised in that holy place.

What a wonderful world we can imagine! Well…

How does all this relate to streams, rivers, forests, mountains?

Perhaps it doesn't directly relate. But, I suspect, Nature is calling us back to class.

Fourteen
The Nature of Humanism

Though I know it must be a little bewildering to some Christian readers, I choose to write about my years as a minister and chaplain and the boundaries I pushed and edges I crossed toward a secular life. This column tells of an evangelical friend, his goodness, his support, and his death. The impact and value of these relationships can endure even after we leave the community of faith. This is true partly because there are other communities, larger, more inclusive and perhaps more meaningful in the bigger picture. Humanism is a world view that not enough people have heard of, let alone seriously considered.

During my years as a Christian minister I was privileged to work side by side with many religious people including folks from most all Christian denominations. I was invited to give sermons in a variety of churches and always had warm welcomes.

My wife and I were close with Steve, an evangelical pastor, who overcame his initial concerns about inter-religious activity to become a strong supporter of cooperative work. He celebrated when Carol and I were married — at a Zen Buddhist retreat, no less.

To everyone's shock and sadness, Steve died the first morning of his retirement. We attended his memorial and offered our comfort to his widow. Such good people.

Steve and I had many differences of opinion when it came to faith, God, and views of the supernatural.

Thankfully we weren't distracted by these disputes but could simply enjoy being colleagues and friends. When I was the county shelter director, Steve was a leading advocate. His church enthusiastically contributed, opening its doors to "the stranger in our midst."

I shake my head thinking of those who build high fences around their beliefs and spend their lives defending their orthodoxy ("correct opinions"). I used to spend lots of time defending my beliefs and trying to save souls before realizing that my soul—if I had one—probably needed more attention than fussing over others. Then, over time, I came to see that no one knows anything about "souls"—besides, who has time to worry about what that means anyway, with so much to be done?

In March of 2017 I addressed the Ethical Humanist Society here in Asheville. My presentation centered on the wise, natural ethical musings of Henry David Thoreau. It was a lively discussion, and I came away feeling that this kind of open exchange of ideas and questions is exactly what we need. In fact, if more religious congregations opened up to these explorations of ideas, maybe there would be a little more understanding between believers and nonbelievers.

There is Humanistic Buddhism and Humanistic Judaism and other "humanized" traditions. But what are the basic principles of Humanism?

The American Humanist Association defines Humanism as "a progressive lifestance that, without supernaturalism, affirms our ability and responsibility to lead meaningful, ethical lives capable of adding to the greater good of humanity."

Since there's no dogmatic creed, various humanist

voices take different approaches to their understanding of Humanist practice. One group defines it as:

"Free of supernaturalism, it recognizes human beings as a part of nature and holds that values—be they religious, ethical, social, or political—have their source in human experience and culture."

Another says:

"This is the only life of which we have certain knowledge and we owe it to ourselves and others to make it the best life possible for ourselves and all with whom we share this fragile planet."

An international coalition presents this statement:

"Humanism is a democratic and ethical lifestance which affirms that human beings have the right and responsibility to give meaning and shape to their own lives."

Some merely summarize Humanism as "Good without a God."

One remarkable thing about Humanists is they have no interest in "converting" anyone to Humanism. There are no evangelists because there is no "belief" to "believe in." People who identify as Humanist or ethical people, are interested in living ethical lives—practicing the good, right and just aspects of being human in human society.

Who could argue with that?

The second talk I gave that month was in Greenville, SC. The Humanist group there hosted me for two hours of great conversation on what I called "Bible Belt and Secular Shoes," another lively conversation on nature, science, and life after faith.

This may sound like I want everyone to become Humanists, but that's not my intent. Becoming more human and humane — practicing more compassionate humanity — doesn't sound so bad, does it? Those who feel threatened by "the secular humanists" might consider this.

Master Kung, the ancient philosopher we call "Confucius," once taught, "It is beautiful to make humaneness one's home. If you do not choose to dwell in humaneness, how can you attain knowledge?" (*Sayings*, chapter 4, verse 1).

Are we at home in our own humanity?

Pastor Steve and I had another clergy friend who calls himself a "Follower of Jesus." Like Steve, he was a good friend, easy to talk with — we would take refreshing walks together. I suspect that was possible because we were friends, worked with some of the same folks in the shelter, and avoided the contentious nature of "god-talk games."

These two pastors and I got along so well because we were naturally humanistic people.

Something to think about.

Fifteen
Climbing Out of Hell

Fear can be a powerful motivator for faith. The thought of causing one's God displeasure or hurting his/her feelings through disobedience can help some keep to the "straight and narrow." The great punishment for not believing has been described for centuries as a burning pit or lake of fire where someone who dares to disbelieve or doubt will suffer torture for eternity. Mainline Christians by and large reject this, yet continually ask for God's forgiveness, assuming God can be hurt, angry, or prepared to "teach a lesson" when disobeyed.

This column addresses the suffering caused this side of the grave by the devilish doctrine of hellfire. One wild naturalist offers a way out of any tyrannical torture chamber.

I thought when my wife and I moved east from the San Francisco Bay Area we would miss some of the most beautiful gifts the West Coast offers: towering redwoods, ancient sequoias, miles of wild Pacific shoreline and the magnificent Sierra mountain range. We do miss these, "The City," and much more. But the good folks of Asheville, the refreshing winds and rains, the star-lit skies and the Green Ridge Mountains (I'm stuck on the green!) are enough to welcome us to a new home.

One thing I've found since we moved to the area is that people are people. No surprise. There are obvious commonalities wherever we go anywhere in America or in the world. Yet, along with the down-deep goodness easily found here, there is some other deeply-rooted stuff that troubles me. West or East, there is great beauty … and great pain.

Not long ago, a student in her seventies told me she was threatened at her church when she was a young girl. This was alarming. I immediately thought she was speaking of abusive behavior. As the father of a daughter I was horrified and wondered who protected her. Then she explained. She felt threatened with punishment—eternal punishment. "Believe, or Else!" was what the little child was told. Now, later in her life, I could still hear a trembling in her voice.

I've heard this for many years, from many brave people who endured these threats—little boys and girls who went to bed with dread, who survived being scared into faith at a very young age, as I was. Though not always so dramatic, the terror of not believing what we're told, that terrible things will happen if we are not faithful enough, casts a long shadow.

There is one four-letter word that scares the heck out of a lot of folks: Hell. The ultimate "time-out," the great prison of perpetual punishment. Either a dark place of separation from anything good, or a boiling lake of fire stirred by your worst nightmares. It used to be that "Go to Hell!" was about the worst thing you could say. Frightening in the extreme.

I studied Theology and the Bible for a long time. Though the Hebrew scriptures (the "old" testament) contains nothing like eternal punishment, the Christian "new" testament developed the concept in some detail. There was a real, physical place—maybe down in the dark, bubbling recesses of the earth—where unbelievers would be thrown. Some have said the word for hell in

Greek, "gehenna," was an endlessly burning garbage heap similar to the awful smelling dump outside the walls of Jerusalem. I don't know. It's nasty—that's all we know.

Here's a blunt summary of the doctrine of hell: "Our God is a God of Love, and our Loving Creator loves us so terribly much that He took the time to construct a horrible place of torture where He will send us forever if we do not love Him in return."

People who believe the Bible literally have to accept and defend this belief as true "biblical theology." More liberal believers who reject this have to either reject the Bible or pick and choose the "nicer" parts and pretend the rest is "old stuff." I used to try that. But thinkers like the Founding Father (and happy heretic) Thomas Paine really got "fired up" about hell. In *The Age of Reason* (1794) he wrote, "Any system of religion that has anything in it that shocks the mind of a child cannot be a true system." Seems like a fair test to me.

Let's bring this a little closer into the light. My daughter is in her 30s now (but still my "little girl"). I love her very much and would never dream of hurting her or causing her to suffer. Would I ever even imagine forcing her to love me by threatening to torture her if she didn't love me back? Heavens, no!

Those of us who dare to question old doctrines like hellfire are accused of attacking faith or persecuting believers. That's nonsense. To raise these valid questions is only threatening to those who are uncomfortable with hearing such a clear and reasonable presentation of their beliefs. Here's the thing: fear-based faith, even couched in the language of love, has left a lot of wreckage along the way.

Like the seasoned student who whispered her painful memories of Sundays long past, there can be a huge sense of relief and liberation in letting go of these destructive beliefs to move forward free of guilt.

As John Muir once mused, if he was tossed down into hell, he would simply find a way to climb out.

Sixteen
Secular Jesus

The Lent-to-Easter and Passover season is always an appropriate time to express some serious wondering. What do we do with the Man of Nazareth? We know what the Church has done with him, but what about those who don't see him as anything more than an influential teacher? As a secular person, it has always seemed to me that many of his "followers" have followed a myth of their own making, which of course leaves room for the rest of us to discover something else about the man – something meaningful and useful for living a good life.

Each year I wish all my Christian friends and family a lovely Lent and energetic Easter! In years past, I frequently led wonderful Lenten and Easter services with uplifting songs, sermons, and symbols of life. At one church where I served as a parish associate, we would wear our white robes and feel a certain thrill when the large wooden cross was brought forward covered in kaleidoscopic colors of spring flowers. Quite beautiful.

As a jail chaplain I remember bringing a flower or two inside to women and men "doing time" in those dark cells. To watch as someone holds and smells the new life of spring, when it may have been a year or more since they even saw some greenery, is a humbling moment. In the jails we would sing folk hymns or spirituals to brighten up the mood for people separated from their husbands, wives, and children.

One year, another chaplain, my friend Rabbi Jerry, invited me to lead a lively Passover-Easter celebration with him.

If the story of human suffering at the hands of injustice has deep spiritual meaning for believers, there are ways that human story can also have a deeper, wider secular meaning.

On my journey away from the cross and the church, I always wondered what would become of Jesus. Once my Lord, Savior and BF, he became an important teacher and model for me—for chaplaincy, teaching, and living a life of compassionate service. But what could the Nazarene be for a nonbeliever? Could the Palestinian rabbi still have something to offer a freethinking secular person?

There are many in the agnostic and atheist community who have no interest whatsoever in the Christ of Christians. A lot of people left the faith for good reasons and simply have no reason to return or even consider that anything they left behind retains any value for them. I understand that. I would never consider going back either.

Yet, Jesus presents an interesting dilemma. Billions say he is the Lord of All and must be worshipped as divine—the incarnated God. And millions of others, who don't call themselves his followers, respect and honor him, seeking to learn from his core teachings.

Maybe this gets to the real issue. What are the "core teachings" of this 2000-year old sage?

It has seemed to me for a very long time that the central issues for Jesus concerned compassion, justice, loving one's neighbor and working for peace. The so-called Sermon on the Mount pretty much sums it up.

And yes, "loving God" is a part of what he taught, but what does that mean? Does it mean believing correctly ("orthodoxy") or practicing a loving life? Some would say it's both. Yet those who emphasize faith and belief sometimes forget that the point is to live better and do good — anyone can say they believe anything. "Show me" is the test, and Jesus seemed to focus on that.

And, of course, we should ask, Which God do you mean to love? A later teaching was fairly basic: "God IS love," So then what? A person acts in a kind and loving manner ... are they a "true believer" or "just" loving? Who gets to judge?

So many questions. Jesus still stirs them up after 2000 years.

Was Jesus a Christian? Of course not. He wasn't Catholic or Protestant or Orthodox or evangelical or any denomination. He certainly never went to church. We know he was Jewish, but not much for synagogues either.

Would he go to church if he was walking around now? Which church? What if he looked like a homeless person, mentally ill, a refugee? Would you let him in?

I don't know, but I suspect the flesh-and-blood Jesus might be drawn to the common people, the outsiders, those of us who only know one world and have to live in it now, who can't be too bothered by some other world beyond the grave, beyond the sky, and beyond reason.

Was Jesus an American? Silly question, let's move on.

Was Jesus a secular person? Now we venture into dangerous territory! As I define it, "secular" simply means grounded in this present world, as opposed to being otherworldly, "spiritual" or "sacred." The Christian world would clearly tell us that definitely,

"No, He was not secular!" He was, they might say, "grounded in another world." To a freethinker that sounds rather nonsensical, but it reminds us of the great divide between Jesus the human being and Jesus who became "The Christ" of the Church.

Imagine for a moment that Jesus indeed was a secular person. What if he died as we all do—returned to the dust of the earth, just like us?

I, for one, would still respect this incredibly wise secular teacher.

Another bridge to cross, Appalachian Mountains

Seventeen
Bridges to and from Belief

This column was the foundation for my sporadic series of interviews with a variety of faith leaders. I've asked these questions of male and female leaders including the director of an Islamic Center, a Baptist pastor, an Episcopal priest, rabbis, ministers, and interfaith leaders. Along the way I've invited a Mormon, an African American evangelist, a Wiccan, several Buddhists – and slipped in a biologist to boot. A few aren't interested and may be reluctant to engage a freethinker, and that's okay. But I think they're missing an opportunity to articulate what it is that holds them back.

What I'm fishing for is a bridge – or maybe I'm fishing from a bridge I think is already built, crossing the gaps and gulfs that divide us by faith. Always curious what ideas I may catch.

How many bridges do you cross each day? Maybe you're walking, cycling or rolling; maybe you're driving or riding along. How many crossings do you make?

How about bridges of the brain, the mind? Do you cross over to new thoughts or ideas? Are there images that span your understanding or the way you imagine the world?

Every town or city I've lived in has been webbed in bridges. I drove across bridges all over Seattle, where I was born and reared. I crossed the San Francisco Bay for many years. Sometimes the smaller bridges were more interesting than the world-famous ones.

Now, here in the Asheville area, you can't go far

without crossing a creek, stream, or river. Not to mention all the spans in the mountain passes.

I suppose it's human to wonder what's across the next bridge. Our curiosity draws us, entices us, almost seduces us, to go over and see the other side. What might be over there? What could I learn if I cross? What would I miss if I don't cross—if I'm too hesitant or afraid?

It seems a natural part of our journey in life to face bridges and the decisions they nudge us to make, the steps to take.

There is a journey to faith, and there is a journey away from faith. Honestly, there are many journeys to many kinds of faith. Which journey one takes depends on the individual and what options are presented. I often think of the bridges that we find to cross—or not. We may move back and forth between beliefs, or between doubt and belief, but until we make a decision to believe or not to believe, we're left with lots of streams, lots of bridges, and lots of questions!

On my own twisting trail into faith and beyond faith, the adventure took me from early Presbyterian to Baptist to Pentecostal and on through evangelical forests. Then the woodlands opened to meadows and mountains where I discovered wider landscapes of the mind and heart. I moved on through ministry, chaplaincy, and nonprofit service. I suppose I could say my viewpoints, like those along the beautiful Blue Ridge Parkway, try to take in all the amazing vistas of the natural world. There is so much to learn from nature, and from each other in our wonderfully diverse world.

Toward this end, I've decided to ask a few local faith leaders some questions. Since I am a secular person who is not anti-religious, and since I value relationships with people of faith, I'm curious how believers interact with those of us who don't share their beliefs.

Here are the questions I'll be presenting to each faith leader:

- How does your faith tradition view nonbelievers (agnostics, atheists, secular people)?

- When you or your congregation have conversations with nonbelievers, is it important to change their minds and convince them of your beliefs?

- Do you view secular worldviews as a threat, a challenge, or an invitation to learn?

- What do you think of nature (and naturalistic views) given your supernatural beliefs?

- Do you think there is value in honest dialogue and cooperative action between people of faith and those without faith? Does this happen in your community?

- Do you have any questions for secular people?

As I receive responses, I will share them here, offering my own reflections.

Some villagers in India weave the thick roots of rubber trees across streams that can be dangerous in the rainy season. One of the oldest bridges has two levels, and villagers are building a third level! They say these spans grow stronger with time.

These living root bridges offer one of the best analogies I can imagine for our communities. Here in Asheville, one excellent model is "Building Bridges," bringing people together to face issues of race. What else can be done to weave roots across barriers, boundaries, and cultural battlefields?

Religions also try to cross the chasms. The World Parliament of Religions first met in Chicago in 1892. The World Council of Churches, founded in 1948, has 348 member churches representing 500 million Christians.

The Interfaith movement has long roots as well. According to the Pluralism Project at Harvard, an association of Christian ministers met in Wichita, Kansas in the 1880s and formed Inter-Faith Ministries. It came to include Jewish, Bahá'í, Muslim, Hindu, and Buddhist members. Interfaith Youth Core has worked with college students all over the world since 2002. And now, some multi-faith groups are including humanists, agnostics, atheists, and freethinkers. Secular Student Alliance came together in 2000.

I wonder: where will this cooperative energy lead, while people weave more living vines and roots together to build sturdier, more inviting bridges we all can enjoy?

Eighteen
Secular Holy Week

My long history with the faith and the founders of traditions gives me some credential to ask uncomfortable questions and push for some rational explanations – without shying away from several major controversies in the Christian narrative. Maybe a secular person can uncover some wider and more relevant meaning to these stories. After all, no one can control the conclusions anyone can arrive at while reading these ancient tales.

Just as I greet Christian friends during their Holy Week with "Happy Easter," I say "Pesach Tov" to my Jewish friends during what are, for the descendants of the Hebrews, the holy days of the Passover season. As it has been for thousands of years, the timeless story of liberation and promise is retold in family and community. It's a profound story with parallels in our contemporary world when we ask, "Who needs freedom today?"

The last days of the Nazarene rabbi are poignant reminders of what can happen when a truth-telling message is silenced by the controllers of truth—or so they think. Yet there is something good hidden in Good Friday, and a surprise awaits the faithful a few days later. The Easter story reminds us that death is not the end. There is joy and hope after the suffering.

For secular people, it is the beautiful season of spring. Native peoples speak of the season of popping trees.

Winter removes her dark, warm, protective cloak and puts on a bright, colorful garment covered in seductive scents (use your own earthy images). April rains replenish clear mountain streams that stir minerals flowing down into dark chocolate rivers spreading enrichment to the land.

Everyone celebrates spring. No matter the faith we have or do not have, no matter the stories we tell, the Great Story is our common story: Nature's playful creativity is active, and we're all a part of the natural saga.

This sounds so Pagan, doesn't it? Well, "pagan" once meant country folk, just as "heathen" used to mean people of the heath or heather. A Wiccan friend of mine would have us up and dancing for the sheer joy of life and earth and being one species among many.

We may not know it and certainly wouldn't admit it, but we all become pagans when the seasons change. If we're perceptive, we sense we're only a small part of one immense universal cycle and show. There's nothing we can do but watch, wonder and participate, if we choose.

I told the Holy Week story for many a year. As a minister I read the passages, sang the hymns, led the prayers, and loved the themes of dark and light, death and life. I've had decades to reflect on these things, and I continue to become reflective as the seasons hop by (they used to roll).

Here's one basic question: Why did Jesus die?

Well, he upset a lot of people. Some say it was "the plan," but I would suggest it had more to do with who his people were—the outcasts, the poorer and more powerless unheard folks ("pagan" perhaps). And not necessarily the religious folk, either. As I've noted, Jesus was not a Christian anyway, and maybe his Jewishness wasn't that important to him either. He was one of us, one of the common people—the "son of man" is how they said it.

And, of course, some accused him of being a heretic infidel, an unpatriotic radical who asked too many questions and offended those who felt he was persecuting them (the same things secular people are accused of today). Saying his message was unpopular is an understatement. What he taught was dangerous, especially to the fearfully faithful.

Here's another question I ponder: Why does it matter if one crucified criminal stumbled out of a tomb a few days later?

I remember being told that if Jesus did not emerge from the tomb after three days—if he did not rise bodily from the grave—the whole Christian faith would crack and crumble apart. We had to defend the Resurrection as if our life depended on it, because our faith surely did. The apostle Paul hammered that into 2000 years of church history.

Yet, if Jesus's revolutionary message, which flip-flopped the world and made justice, compassion, and truth-telling to the powerful and pious the central point, do we need him to perform miracles—capped off with rising from the dead—to get the point and get busy?

One last question: Does Easter today have much to do with those long-ago events?

Like our computers, our stories need updates. Passover reboots us: there are enslaved people today—captive in body or mind—who could use an encouraging story that tells them their lives matter and others stand with them. Easter restarts us: there are people today in the pain of poverty or hopelessness—who face suffering and death—who could use a new narrative. Not one that promises another world or dramatic miracles, but a reasonable message that they are not alone as they pass through nature's cycles and circles.

To all those who celebrate Pesach, Easter, or simply the coming of the spring, I wish the goodness of the season to all.

Nineteen
Awakening to Sabbath

Popular culture gives an endless amount of material for tracing the edges of secularism and spirituality. Quite often it appears that media drives our beliefs because it's where we turn for stories that matter. Whether we believe in a deity or not, there is a kind of transcendence that we feel when we're taken far into space or deep into our own bodies and brains. Sharing some insights from Oliver Sachs's end-of-life wisdom generates this secular discussion of "sabbath," since the concept of rest and regeneration is not owned or managed by religion.

The powerful film *Awakenings*, starring Robin Williams and Robert De Niro, was meaningful during my early years as a chaplain with people having mental and physical challenges. Based on the book, the film tells the true story of Oliver Sachs, a neurologist working with people in a New York City hospital who have, as some would say, "broken brains." He finds ways of bringing them out of the faraway fog within, back to the reality of life.

Oliver Sachs died in 2015. Two weeks before his death he published a short essay on "Sabbath" (in the book *Gratitude*). Growing up in an Orthodox Jewish home, Sachs moved away from the rituals and the religious beliefs of his physician parents but not from his love of family, respecting their deep commitment to tradition.

In his last weeks, Sachs was very weak—every

breath was difficult. Near death he reflected on the meaning of Sabbath:

"I find my thoughts, increasingly, not on the supernatural or spiritual but on what is meant by living a good and worthwhile life—achieving a sense of peace within oneself. I find my thoughts drifting to the Sabbath, the day of rest." He concludes, "Perhaps [it's] the seventh day of one's life as well, when one can feel that one's work is done, and one may, in good conscience, rest."

Sadly, Oliver Sachs was rejected by his mother at eighteen when he told his parents he "liked boys." His mother told him, "I wish you had never been born."

Some who suffer this kind of traumatic rift grow to hate religion and avoid religious people. Families can be painfully torn apart; wounds may never heal. The synagogue or church, mosque or temple becomes a symbol of separation rather than a sanctuary. Promises of "salvation" (deliverance, healing) seem empty—a call or demand for a person to be rescued from who they are. Such salvation feels more like condemnation or even damnation. And some are told exactly that.

Yet many former believers who become agnostic or atheist choose to hold onto an appreciation for the gifts of the faith community. As a member of The Clergy Project (TCP), I hear quite a few ministers and some rabbis express a deep love for the community they once served or continue to serve. Though TCP members are nonbelievers now, there is a natural, humanistic commitment to helping people in any way we can. This is living proof that people can live loving, fulfilling lives and be, as we like to say, Good without God.

Awakening happens in many unexpected ways. We may see ourselves in a "new light" or learn a fresh truth about our world. We may fall in love or delight in a new friendship. We may witness the birth of a child or watch with wonder as heat-lightning illumines the night sky. We may even face dying or the death of a loved one with a renewed appreciation for each day's breath.

As Buddhists say, waking up is the essence of our "buddha-nature." To be "buddha" is to be awake—fully alive. Who doesn't want that? A Christian may see himself or herself as a "Christ-in-one" who lives the message of being "sent to serve." For Jews, like Oliver Sachs, waking up can happen while saying the Shema, dancing with the Torah, or performing a "mitzvah": an act of service.

For secular freethinkers, small and great awakenings can make every day a kind of sabbath—rejuvenating days, even moments, when things come into focus, when clarity opens our eyes and *Life is good!* (We don't need t-shirts to tell us).

In my jail chaplaincy days, I would sometimes wander onto a cellblock when most inmates were sleeping. It might have been the middle of the day for me, but when all you have is artificial light and the sun never warms your face, why not just sleep? Some told me they were "sleeping off my sentence." I understood.

At times I would find one man or one woman awake so I would stop and crouch down to speak with them through the cold steel bars. Some of the best and most meaningful conversations happened in those quiet moments. There was a touch of honesty, of trust, and maybe something called "grace," if that can mean human acceptance without judging. An elderly

African American man asked for a prayer; a young Muslim woman asked for a Qur'an; an evangelical teen requested a visit from her pastor; a gay man was lonely; a tearful Latina missed her family.

A chaplain listens, chooses to be fully present—simply "there"—and that's just about all that matters. Those moments are sabbath as they are awakening.

Twenty
Peeves, Goats, and the Faith of Children

Young people are naturally influenced in their beliefs by adults – who often present them with only one option. That can be irritating to one who believes in opening minds rather than closing them. I find it much better to approach the subject with a touch of humor without too much peevishness.

I have some pet peeves, and I know you do too. I have no idea what a "peeve" is, but I know some have been my pets for a long time. Some of my pet peeves "get my goat," if you know what I mean.

The Urban Dictionary defines "get your goat" as "to annoy you to the point of getting [upset]." It explains: "The goat is a metaphor for your state of peacefulness. When your goat is with you, you are calm and collected. When your goat is stolen, you become angry and upset."

A "peeve" is apparently from peevish and means "a cause of annoyance." When I encounter someone's pet on a trail whose owner lets it bark at me, jump on me, or even nip at my leg, I'd say that was certainly an annoyance.

Peevish. Annoyed. Upset? However lightly I'm expressing displeasure, I'm actually serious about something here.

Reading through some writings of school kids I was both impressed and troubled. Young people like writing about nature and their families, sports teams, animals, and whatever delights them. There is a wondrous sense of imagination, humor, and some very deep thought.

What children say or write about their religious faith should give us pause. One fifth-grade girl states, "The first person I love is God." She goes on to mention her family but then ends with this jarring line: "Without my faith, I would be giving up all the time and I wouldn't be happy anymore." To hear a young child be so self-assured that without her faith she would be unhappy and give up—that's hard to hear.

Where did she learn that?

A sixth-grader said the three most important things in his life were his favorite football team, his family, and God. He says that God is important because "he gives me someone to pray to and love," but goes on to say, "He also tries to protect me from the fires of hell."

Who teaches that to a child?

A third example. A little girl writes that she loves her dog, her grandmother, and her God. She believes "He is the creator and he made me along with all of the people in the world." Not too alarming. But then she states with confidence, "He is our savior and the one that saved our lives from eternal sin." According to this young mind, people "just need some faith!"

I wonder, will this child learn from others, hear other voices and find there are other ways of understanding the world?

Thank goodness she ends with these words: "The world is perfect to me, and I love the things in it. I am excited to discover new things that are important to me."

What a relief. I needed to hear that. There is hope in the next generation.

After all, isn't that the fertile promise of childhood blooming into adulthood — to discover new things that are important to us, to others, to living in a world full of playful, inquisitive children who grow up to be curious, wondering adults?

What really gets my peeved goat is when children are not given the opportunity at an early stage of their development to really use their minds; when kids are discouraged from valuing their own critical thinking at the same time they value the joy of pure fun and exploration of the bigger world out there.

Rote repetition and ritual can disrespect a child's "god-given" intellect. Someday they'll ask questions. Then what?

Have you ever seen those videos of very small children reciting passages of the Bible or the Qur'an? Have you seen children praying together or singing religious songs? In my opinion, there is nothing inherently wrong or destructive about these things, if a child is respected enough to allow them the opportunity to see and hear and experience alternative expressions of faith and be presented with the choice to have no faith.

When a young person is taught that there is only one faith, one way to view God, then how will they ever learn to appreciate other faiths and other viewpoints? When a child is taught they will be punished for eternity if they are not a "good little believer," how is that not a fear-based faith?

Of particular concern to my goat: how will a child have respect for a secular person who doesn't believe?

I may be an old goat with a small herd of pet peeves, but I'm not sheepish about my need to chew on these things.

Fuzzbuzzer in rhododendron, Asheville, NC

Twenty-one
Shoes On, Shoes Off

This is not the best period of time for a person to identify as Muslim in America. Through sheer "heroic ignorance," many people simply don't like Islam or Muslims and want them to leave or stay out of the "land of the free." My wife and I have Muslim friends and know them as good, loving people. I have issues with much that Islam teaches (as with other religions), but taking off shoes with the faithful can be humbling for anyone.

This column presented the first in my occasional series of interviews with faith leaders. We hear an impressive voice of welcoming. Though, unfortunately, most may never make the effort to attend a "masjid" prayer, I encourage it, even for secular people. When you sense the humanity, the rhythm of chant and body, there is a peacefulness evident in the practice of "salaam" – peace.

When I hear someone making critical comments about a specific group of people—whether it's about ethnicity, sexual orientation, political or religious affiliation—I have a few standard questions: Have you met such a person? What does your labeled friend think and feel? What are you learning about [that group]?

Pretty well stops the conversation. It's easy for us to generalize about "those people" until we actually make the effort to meet and get to know a few of them—to listen and learn.

This is how I felt when Carol and I visited the Islamic Center of Asheville. We both have friends and colleagues in the Muslim community and wanted to show support for our Muslim neighbors here.

Arriving at the small neighborhood masjid (mosque) we were warmly welcomed by smiling adults and children greeting us with, "Thank you for coming!" We removed our shoes and entered the well-lit room and sat on the carpeted floor with a roomful of members and guests listening to a sermon by the president of the Islamic Center, Khalid Bashir. Reading from his notes, Mr. Bashir was presenting a slow, deliberate explanation of Muslim teaching on equality and justice drawn from Qur'an passages he read in Arabic and English.

"Oh you who believe, Be staunch in justice, witnesses for Allah, even though it be against yourselves or your parents or your kindred, whether the case be of a rich person or a poor one, for Allah is nearer unto both" (surah [chapter] 4:135).

He went on to quote from surah 49:13: "O mankind, Lo! We have created you male and female, and have made you nations and tribes that you may know one another."

When the time for prayer arrived, I slipped out to give more room for the stream of worshippers pouring in. Many people from all over the area were quietly waiting on the grass. I stepped closer to a young man standing by himself and asked if he had been to a mosque before. Shyly he whispered that he had not, and said, "I didn't even know there were Muslims in Asheville."

I spoke with Mr. Bashir by phone later and he told me the community doesn't always have an imam (teacher) but he and several other volunteers speak on the Qur'an each week. The center was opened in 2005 and there are now 75 to 100 families who represent numerous nations around the world. Bashir came to the U.S. from Pakistan.

Some have a feeling of uncertainty about the current immigration chaos. However, members feel the good support from other faith groups in the Asheville area and are pleased that many people show a desire to learn.

Bashir calmly assured me that their members don't force their beliefs or teachings on non-religious or other religions. They are committed to showing respect for individual decisions. Regarding secular people, he said he doesn't criticize or look down on others for their belief or lack of belief.

When I asked Mr. Bashir if there was anything he would want "Asheville" to know, he answered that Muslims have been here a long time and wish to live in peaceful co-existence with all neighbors. He invites anyone with concerns or questions to come to them directly rather than to the media, because it is very important to speak with "knowledgeable sources" regarding Islam or the Qur'an.

The public is welcome to visit the Asheville masjid (mosque) on Fridays to hear a sermon from 1:30 to 2:00 p.m. Prayers begin at 2:00 (note that women enter by a separate door and sit in a separate section—feel free to ask about that). Everyone takes their shoes off, and people are welcome to sit and observe or kneel for prayer.

The image that stays in my mind is the young man standing alone outside. He was invited in, removed his shoes, and entered quietly and respectfully.

Maybe that's one key that opens the door of understanding. Make the effort to go, to learn, to meet people you may be curious about, maybe even fearful of. Leave the fear—one human to another—ask questions or just be quiet and respectful.

As a nonbeliever (some might say "infidel" or "heretic"), I welcome the opportunity to sit, stand or even pray (or sit silently) with all peaceable people who teach justice, equality and hospitality.

My American Muslim colleagues are not particularly interested in convincing me that their faith is the best, or that I should believe. If they, or believers of any religion, choose to follow ancient teachings of equality and justice, secular folk like me can respectfully meet them at that door any day—and even remove our shoes.

Twenty-two
Children and Their Questions of Faith

In a part of the country where Sunday schools thrive, where many children are raised with a belief in one God, one church, one faith, it seems necessary to raise something else: questions. I'm as gentle as can be when it comes to kids, but I also think it's critical that they hear strong, rational adult voices presenting choices for young minds. A niece and a nephew were visiting and I decided to try something new: asking them what they thought about faith and God and atheists. At first they grew very quiet. After all, whoever asks a child what they honestly think about these things? Their responses were priceless.

"And a child shall lead them." This famous line from the prophet Isaiah (chapter 11) is a favorite for preaching "the peaceful kingdom." All creatures living in harmony: the wolf with the lamb, the leopard with the goat, the calf with the lion, the cow with the bear, the ox with the adder. A startling scene, like something from *The Chronicles of Narnia* or *The Trilogy of the Rings*.

Though this is Hebrew scripture, some want us to believe this is a prophecy of the Christian savior—Jesus—the only one "the spirit of the Lord shall rest" upon; that he is the only one who will "judge the poor and the meek" with righteousness. Of course, they may leave out the part that says "he shall strike the earth with the rod of his mouth and with the breath of his lips he shall kill the wicked." Not exactly a peaceable vision.

This gets me thinking less of theology and ancient scrolls and more about what it would be like to listen and learn from children—the younger voices. In the great distracting debates over religious faith, adults often neglect to pay attention to what the young people are thinking or what they feel about beliefs that unite or divide the world.

I asked my North Carolina niece and nephew what they thought about some of these things. It is instructive to pay attention to their responses (especially since their mother is a teacher and their aunt is a minister).

I asked, "What does the word 'God' mean to you? What comes to mind?" My eleven-year-old nephew became very thoughtful. "Loving," was all he said. When we came back to this later he added, "Grateful." He clarified, "God is grateful and we're grateful."

Separately, my thirteen-year-old niece answered, "Someone to look up to." Then she smiled and said it was like "a floating person."

"What do you think of church?" I asked. My nephew said, "Quiet." My niece said, "Singing."

Asking if kids at their public school talk about faith, they both answered without hesitation, "No." My nephew added that if students did talk about their faith, it might cause trouble. I explained that it's ok for kids to talk about faith as long as it's respectful and not disruptive.

Then I asked if they learn about religion in school? My niece said her teachers were "not allowed" to talk about faith, but they teach about religions all around the world—she named Christian, Jewish, Buddhist, Muslim. Both kids seemed to understand the basic idea of separation of religion and state.

Something my nephew said made me curious. He said there was a girl in his class from another country who wears a head covering. He eats lunch with her sometimes. He's not sure what religion she is or why she wears the scarf. He says some classmates are "scared to ask" her about it. I encouraged him to ask.

What about people who don't believe in God? Their answers were encouraging. "It doesn't really matter — we're all just people." "It doesn't bother me — it's a free country!"

"Do you think there's a place called 'heaven' or 'hell?'" Thankfully, the eleven-year-old simply said he doesn't think about it. The teenager thinks heaven is "a happy place, somewhere in the sky" and hell is an "evil or bad place — down in the ground where the lava is." Now there's the classic image! I asked her where she learned that. "Books and movies." No surprise.

For fun, I asked if there was *any* question they could ask in church, what would it be? The younger one said, "Why is world peace not a thing?" I asked for more. "Why is there so much terror?" Wow. The older one took it more lightly: "Why do we only get communion every once in a while?" I smiled, looking puzzled. She said, "So I can eat!" Here she giggled, as only a precocious girl can.

I couldn't resist asking, "What does nature mean to you?" (I'm fascinated by the ways we conflate god-talk and nature-talk). The elementary school student said, "Interesting — all the colors and sounds all around us. Every part of nature is important. It can be dangerous, so we need to be careful." The middle-schooler rattled off: "outdoors, hiking, exploring, animals, trees."

They were much more animated and bright-eyed talking about nature. Of course, in my secular view, this was delightful.

These are deep questions for any age and I'm proud of my niece and nephew for being so honest. It makes me wonder, what if children were our leaders, our teachers—and maybe they are.

Twenty-three
Was Jesus Ever Wrong?

The answer of course is an emphatic "No!" — at least if you feel that your faith depends on defending a "perfect" human being who lived and died several thousand years ago. There are those who feel that certain subjects are off limits, and they feel disrespected when we raise uncomfortable questions. It seems at times they are most afraid of offending God, who apparently cannot defend Godself.

I believe we owe it to ourselves to put all questions, no matter how unsettling, on the table for free discussion. This can be done respectfully. Yet those who are easily hurt and offended may find any open discussions, particularly about those they revere, unacceptably bothersome. I don't think we can let that silence the exercising of our minds.

A number of years ago when I was still attempting to save the world (to make the whole planet believe just what I believed) I was desperate to convince everyone I met that Jesus was the answer (even if they hadn't asked the question). For me and my fellow crusaders, Jesus was everything—he was God and Lord and Savior and Friend. Nothing mattered more than my personal relationship with Him and nothing was more important than bringing anyone and everyone to "accept Jesus."

There was something quite wonderful about this worldview, I must admit. It made life quite simple. It was a God-or-nothing way of life, gave me lots of friends and opened the way for me to be a leader in my youth group, in Campus Crusade (now called Cru), and, later, in ministry. Like many exclusive worldviews, there was a dark side. I had no friends outside the circle of evangelistic faith and I was constantly under pressure to preach the good news before it was too late. And it was getting late. We "knew" Jesus was returning soon and we didn't want to be caught shirking our sacred responsibility to lead as many to Christ as we could (including my Jewish girlfriend and heathen classmates). We were heartsick with the thought that if we missed sharing the "good news" with someone our Loving God would have to torture them for eternity in hell. That's a heavy burden for a teen.

I've talked a lot about my own journey, but it's important background to what I'm looking at today. It never would have crossed my mind in those younger days that any of it could be wrong. That would be a terrible sin to think about. Later, in seminary years, we found out we weren't alone in asking the hard questions. It was no longer a sin, but actually expected, that we would wrestle with the most troubling aspects of faith. I'll always be grateful for that.

Now, as a secular person, I think it's wise and honest to listen to people's most disturbing questions and raise some of my own. We have nothing to fear from speaking our doubts and questions—admitting we don't know all the answers is healthy and fairly essential.

One stunning puzzle has circled back for a long time now: Was Jesus ever wrong? As a great respected teacher with an expanding group of followers, his instructions covered a lot of ground. He spoke about human society—poor and rich; God and government as well as personal things like faith, suffering, ethical conduct, and much more. He also told stories about trees, plants, and animals. He talked about earth and heaven and hell. This all assumes we can know what he "really" said. We don't have even one original source—and let's not forget, unlike many teachers, he never wrote one word that got published.

We read about Jesus as a pre-teen disobeying his parents to sneak off to argue in the temple. That seems disrespectful in several ways ("honor your father and mother"). During his ministry he curses a fig tree, shows violent anger while "cleansing the temple" with a whip, tells a woman she is like a dog who can only eat crumbs under the table, and allows his disciples to buy weapons (swords).

Some could take issue with his preference for the poor ("blessed are the poor" who inherit the kingdom, "give all to the poor and follow me"), the unfairness in his story of paying laborers who work an hour the same as those who worked all day, and his statement that some standing before him would still be alive to see him return from the sky. I'm not talking about "contradictions" here. An ancient book, written by many people over hundreds of years, is bound to have contradictions. What these examples circle back to is the main question: Was Jesus ever wrong? Could he have made mistakes? Not just mistakes in the story about him, but could he have messed up sometimes, been in error or confused?

I was taught in Theology and Christology classes that Jesus was "fully human and fully God." This always struck me as similar to the creedal claim that "Three equals One" (the "trinity"). It's hard to make sense of that, and theologians tell us it's not supposed to make sense—we should accept it "by faith."

Personally I don't think we need to accept anything that seems nonsensical and "just believe." If you're a believer, that seems to disrespect a God who made the brain.

If Jesus was a real human being, why couldn't we say he was less than perfect—he was like us. That way, even non-Christians and nonbelievers could "accept" this marvelously imperfect man.

Twenty-four
Welcoming People Not Like You

In my conversations with leaders of different faith communities, there are few surprises, yet overall I'm encouraged to hear thoughtful responses that welcome the conversation. This rabbi was comfortable with me and easy to converse with. It always makes me wonder why more people aren't engaging these questions and conversations in a variety of settings, especially in the faith communities themselves. On the other hand, I understand the wariness of nonbelievers. I can well remember encountering that over the course of my own journey.

When I was the street chaplain in Marin County, CA, my office was initially in a small room tucked behind the altar of the sanctuary in a large Protestant church. Many people living outside without a home came in to talk, pick up a blanket or bus ticket, or simply rest. We started a "Wellness" group in one church meeting space and then an art and poetry group. As time went on, the chaplaincy hosted meals, and the church let us use the kitchen. For the most part, the pastor and congregation were supportive.

Unfortunately, the good relationship was challenged when some of our unhoused friends began sleeping in the doorways of the church. After a contentious meeting it was decided "No Trespassing" signs would go up over the doors and the police would be called if anyone saw someone sleeping on the property. One elderly doctor asked his fellow parishioners, "What ever happened to 'forgive us our trespasses'?" I'll always remember how encouraging that was to hear.

I tell this story because of my engaging conversation with Rabbi Batsheva Meiri of Congregation Beth HaTephila in Asheville. I asked her a series of questions about the interface of her religious community and the secular world. Rabbi Meiri gave me a lot to think about, and my guess is that readers will appreciate some of her provocative responses.

The congregation has been here since the 1890s, reflecting the Jewish community's deep roots in WNC. Along the way, the congregation met in an old church before building their own sanctuary in the 1940s. More recent renovations encircle the old facility. Having a history connected to a church structure, the synagogue now enjoys sharing space from time to time with several local churches. As Rabbi Meiri puts it, there are "longstanding, neighboring friendships" that have evolved.

The synagogue practices an "audacious hospitality" that shows a commitment to "diversity and connections," evidenced in their participation with Room in the Inn, a program that offers temporary housing, meals, and assistance to homeless women throughout the year, as well as pulpit exchanges with a UCC church, St. Mark's Lutheran, and St. Mary's Episcopal.

During a 2016 spate of bomb threats to Jewish centers here and across the nation, Rabbi Meiri says the "community stood together to affirm our relationships." With the increase of anti-Semitism and hate crimes, she feels a strong sense of support from Asheville. I heard similar sentiment from Khalid Bashir of the Islamic Center.

When asked how the Jewish tradition views nonbelievers (agnostics, atheists, and secular people), she replied, "Judaism is less about beliefs than about action." It's not about creeds (the "I-Believes"); the concern is to discover the "great commonalities" because "we can't claim 'Truth' with a capital T." She went on to explain there is "no need for answers" but to "let the questions stand." We can grapple with uncomfortable ideas and issues but "it can be comfortable to struggle together." This approach "canonizes opposing views." Isn't that a stunning statement!

Reform Judaism has no interest in changing the minds of non-Jews. There is "no need for singularity of opinion" because there is "respect for one another as valuable human beings." As long as there is no intent to be hurtful, different views, unsettling as they can be, are addressed in the context of a central question: "What is the forward action?" If people can work side by side for a clear and constructive purpose, belief is not the issue and it need not divide.

Rabbi Meiri agreed that building bridges is important, and it seems Congregation Beth HaTephila is "weaving the living roots and branches" of those bridges every day. Already deeply involved in interfaith work, the synagogue never tries to "push God" on others but seeks to "hold space for people to raise themselves."

As for nature and naturalistic thought, Rabbi Meiri offered some wisdom that could have come straight from John Muir: "Nature is miraculous; we don't need something outside of natural laws to be amazed." She said we could call it "spiritual," but "amazing" is just as good. This might be a good lesson for us to mull over here in the beauty of the mountains and hollers, no matter what views we hold.

My conversation with Rabbi Meiri concluded with something I might hold as a thread to carry along this trail of bridges as we hear from other faith leaders. She said that "no one is excluded because they aren't a member"; she explained that it is the right thing "to be welcoming of people not like you."

The conclusion is that real community lies in "unity of purpose" — that including more people, with various voices, makes sense, and makes us all stronger, and maybe better. The rabbi and I agree, I think, that healthier communities look forward, expecting good things as people find ways of living their amazement.

Twenty-five
Faith Lessons from Frederick Law Olmsted

We all enjoy a good story, especially one that has some meaning for us. In my writing I often refer to a hero or heroine in secular history and how they related to religion in their personal lives. For many readers I think this approach shows that great things have been done and are being done today by people who choose not to believe in the supernatural. Great people do not need God. Living near the massive Biltmore Estate, the largest private home in America, I've been fascinated with the genius of Frederick Law Olmsted. Creative minds can inspire us all, faith or no faith.

Genius of Place is Justin Martin's fascinating biography of Frederick Law Olmsted, America's first and foremost landscape architect. Olmsted's incredibly imaginative mind gave us New York City's Central Park, the U.S. Capitol grounds, the campuses of Stanford, Amherst, and American University, and many other sites. In fact, Olmsted designed more than thirty major city parks and lent his visionary ideas for iconic public spaces spanning across the country as far as Golden Gate Park in San Francisco. His commitment to open spaces as community treasures open to all continues to inspire architects, including Peter Walker who designed the World Trade Center memorial site.

I was surprised to learn that Olmsted was a correspondent for the earliest issues of *The New York*

Times. The series of articles he wrote about the South, first published in 1861 as *The Cotton Kingdom*, reveal the horrendous practices of slavery. Though he initially felt a gradual end of the institution was best, he changed his mind when he witnessed first-hand the inhuman abuses. During one of his assignments he took a stagecoach through North Carolina: his experiences made him a "red-hot abolitionist."

Olmsted's social consciousness is reflected in his natural designs. The long, winding and wild entrance to the Biltmore Estate, welcoming to any and all, entices and teases until one comes out from the forest, through the gate, and is given the final gift of the spectacular view. And the view is much more than the massive house! Around and beyond the chateau are forest, rolling green hills, streams, lakes, and the distant Smoky Mountains — America the Beautiful. Biltmore, like Central Park, was "intended to furnish healthful recreation for the poor and the rich, the young and the old, the vicious and the virtuous." I imagine one day, when the estate becomes a national monument, accessible and affordable to the masses, Olmsted's intent for his landscape will be even more pronounced and appreciated.

I wasn't too surprised to discover that Frederick Law Olmsted wasn't much of a religious man. Born in Hartford, Connecticut, Frederick was pressured to "get converted" in the fiery revivals of the 1820s and '30s. He prayed hard, felt "God's fever," and had a strong physical reaction to the hours of preaching. "In the weeks afterward," his biographer Martin explains, "he concluded that it was simply a headache."

Martin goes on to say, "Like his father, Olmsted

appeared constitutionally unable to fall 'under conviction'." Frederick didn't reject religion completely, but "he found himself unable to meet a strict standard of faith in a highly organized setting. The revival didn't stick."

For those of us who have experienced revivals and evangelistic "crusades" or even the dramatic passion of a Bible-waving preacher in the pulpit, Olmsted's early story is both familiar and affirming. For a young person to "feel the spirit" and "accept the Lord" before hearing of any reasonable options does a disservice to both belief and brain. However, it can also be a kind of rite of passage—and right of passage—for us to choose faith with youthful exuberance, but later in life choose, with a great sense of relief, to "Let Go and Let Good." To accept an earthly Love instead of a heavenly Lord, to take responsibility for rational decisions rather than merely assent to a "just believe" mentality, can bring a great feeling of liberation and contentment. The architect from Connecticut seemed to sense that, and it showed in his creative thought and work.

Frederick Olmsted went on to become a "scientific farmer" in upstate New York, Connecticut, and Staten Island. His intensely close work with the land and his significant and interesting friendships (including with Charles Brace, who studied at Union Seminary in New York and then, in 1860, introduced Henry Thoreau to a radical new book just arrived in the New World— Charles Darwin's *The Origin of Species*; see Ch. 35), made Olmsted into a reformer with ideas as well as landscapes. It may be important to keep that reforming connection in mind, since this reformation in freethinking, unlike religious reformation, thrives on a revival of reason and a deep love of nature.

I recently took a West Coast friend to the Biltmore Estate. We parked down in the gardens and walked up to the house through the lattice path, then wound up the hill to the terrace where the expansive scene rolls out before you. We both felt the beauty of the natural world and could almost ignore the mammoth structure Vanderbilt called home. We did go in of course, but it was the garden, the forests, the twisted vines, the budding of early spring that most caught our attention. Sure, the house is magnificent. But Olmsted's radical freethinking vision is still at play, in the living, greening genius of place.

French Broad River, Hot Springs, NC

Twenty-six
Rivers across the Religious Landscape

Once again using images from my personal story, this selection hopes to convey a lesson of life through nature. Simple; simply profound. Not some sweet parable or miraculous leap to universal conclusions, but utilizing a common image – like a river or glass of water – to pick up something educational, even wise. This reveals my longtime sense that John Muir was right: the more we go into nature, the more we will understand ourselves. And, as Muir discovered, beauty was really the best way to think of anything divine.

Reading the latest issue of *Nature Conservancy* magazine, I turned a page to a stunning graphic. The image shows the major watersheds of the United States. Displayed in vibrant colors, the land appears alive, like arteries lacing across continental skin—a living creature pulsating with life.

Staring at this picture brought a smile to my face. When we see the country, or the world, undivided by states and borders, highways and cities, it's not hard to see the very real interconnections that weave us together.

Springs, creeks, streams, rivers. The flow of water ought to be a continual reminder we are watery beings swimming in currents of air on a saturated sphere in space. Whatever the extremes—floods and droughts, thunderstorms or blue skies—the constant is liquid life or lack of it.

Growing up along the shores of the Puget Sound, salt water ran in my veins. With both the Cascade and Olympic mountain ranges in view every day, we were aware that all the soaking rain kept an endless supply of fresh water literally flowing down into our faucets. It was obvious why Washington (washing-a-ton) was called the "Evergreen State."

The Conservancy magazine startled me again with a less dramatic image: a glass of water. Below it, these words poured into my eyes: "Hydrologists estimate that if all the water on Earth filled a 5-gallon bucket, just one drop of it would represent the clean, fresh water accessible to humans." One drop. That should be a cold splash in the face to wake up every community on the big blue-green globe.

Speaking of waking up ... what do religion and faith have to say about the precious gift of H_2O? Traditions talk of rivers (Jordan, Ganges, Nile, etc.), of "raining blessings" and purifying baptism. Jesus spoke of "living water" and one story says he even walked on a lake.

The biblical view of heaven is not merely an eternal megachurch service in a golden city in the sky. A river runs right through with the roots of the Tree of Life stretching into the celestial waters. I would choose the river instead of the service, but that's just me.

Water has been a central symbol in religion for good reason. The magazine article makes it crystal clear: we are made of water; we depend on water and, there isn't much of it to share—yet, share we must.

I can't really believe this needs to be said in 2017, but there is no such thing as a Sufi spring, a Christian creek, a Jewish stream or an Atheist river. You need fresh clean water; I need fresh clean water. Believer or nonbeliever, God or no God, water truly is life. In one sense, Jesus was right: there is living water, but it doesn't have to be spiritual or miraculous. Hindus in India worship rivers as gods and goddesses—but the rivers aren't Hindu rivers.

Here in WNC we have beautiful watersheds—gifts of the wild green mountains. These vital lands are fed by the French Broad and the Swannanoa, the Pigeon, Little Tennessee, and Tuckasegee. Where I grew up, even as a child I could pronounce the names of rivers in the language of the First Nations: Snohomish, Stillaguamish, Skykomish, Skagit. Later in life I crossed the mighty Columbia to discover the pure streams of the Sierras: the Sacramento, the American, the Merced, Tuolumne, and many others.

One day I drove across a network of rivers including the Catawba to visit the International Civil Rights Museum in Greensboro with my wife, her sister, and mother. (If you haven't been, I highly recommend it.) The museum is located on the site of the Woolworth's store where four African American young men sat at the lunch counter in 1960 igniting a movement to integrate lunchrooms across the nation. Like a flood of freedom, a relentless river of human rights flowed through communities where dams of bigotry held back many from simply sitting on a stool to order a glass of water.

One drop. A drop in a bucket. But how great a value is that drop.

Rivers—of the land and of the mind—make us who we are. We all live in one watershed, so to speak, nourished by many rivers.

Once in a while it might be good for us to think of the nation, or the world, as One Watershed or One River or maybe just One Drop. How will we draw from that limited supply? Who controls it and who will have access? Forget arguing over "global warming" and "climate change"—our rallying cry should be: "Save the Drop."

Twenty-seven
Here We Sit: 500 Years of Reformation

The history of religion is long and complex, the history of Christendom a labyrinth that can leave you lost, confused or just plain frustrated. Like all the splinters that split from the Reformation tree, Reformed and Lutheran groups each believed they were God's special tribe. I read John Calvin in my Reformed seminary but never really learned to like him; however, a committee would not ordain me until I quoted him and verbally bowed in allegiance. Thank goodness there are many in both camps today who have found ways of living together and learning from each other. Still, the "reforming spirit" remains elusive for the vast majority.

The year 1517 was the historic moment when a German monk named Martin Luther hammered his debatable demands onto the heavy wooden doors of the Wittenberg Cathedral. But other than Lutherans, who cares?

I think his story can still stir honest debate in the spiritual and secular communities today.

Luther (1483-1546) studied law before deciding to become a monk. One account says he made this decision when a violent thunderstorm scared him so much he vowed to join a monastery if he survived. His father wasn't happy because Martin was giving up a promising career in law. After studying Theology and Scripture at the university he received his doctorate in 1512.

As the famous story goes, Luther became angry

when he heard that a Dominican monk was selling "indulgences" (forgiveness of sins). Among other things that irritated him about the Church, this one tipped the scales. He sent copies of his Ninety-Five Theses to Church leaders to stir up academic debate, and (possibly) posted them on the cathedral blog—that is, the front door.

He expected honest debate. His bullet points begin with an open invitation: "Out of love for the truth and from desire to elucidate it, the Reverend Father Martin Luther ... intends to defend the following statements and to dispute on them.... Therefore he asks that those who cannot be present and dispute with him orally shall do so in their absence by letter."

His protest included affirmations of the Bible as the only source of authority and salvation by grace alone, not works. He was not against the pope, just the nonsensical abuses of "authorities."

In 1521 the agitated professor was excommunicated as a heretic. In a dramatic scene he was told to repudiate his writings yet courageously stated, "Here I stand. I can do no other. God help me. Amen." (Standing up to orthodoxy is also a main element of the Freethought tradition).

Luther spent the next years hiding out, then agitating even more, marrying a former nun, and getting himself in deeper theses. In 1530 his followers presented a statement of protesting beliefs in Augsburg which became the standard for Lutheranism for centuries.

In seminary we didn't study the Augsburg Confession: it is not included in *The Book of Confessions* that we studied. We were proudly "Reformed" (Presbyterian, following the Calvinist tradition) rather than "Protestant" (Lutheran). Though both grew out of the historical Reformation—breaking away from the Catholic Church—Calvin and Luther mixed like holy oil and holy water.

Strange as it seems, one of the most divisive elements of the whole history of Christianity is how to understand what's happening with "The Elements"—the bread and wine of the Eucharist, Communion, the Lord's Supper. The holy meal is supposed to be all about unity, yet continues to divide not just Catholic and Protestant, but Lutheran and Presbyterian and others. Luther couldn't get along with other reformers like the Swiss Zwingli and the French "General of Geneva," John Calvin. None of them could agree whether the bread was "really" the body of Christ or a figure of speech or the "presence" of Christ. There could be no peace over pieces of the Prince of Peace.

Meanwhile, of course, people need bread. There are hungry people and also people hungry to see some unity and love in the world. While theological debates drone on, and "irrelevant" becomes graffiti on heavy, locked, and well-defended church doors, the world moves on. Though "Reformed, always Reforming" was a mantra we repeated in seminary, the "real presence" of that is sometimes hard to see (for example, it took only about 450 years for Protestants to ordain women).

My maternal grandmother, Emma, was a German Lutheran. I still have her *Gesangbuch fur Kirche, Schule und Haus* (*Songbook for Church, School and House*) given to her in 1907. I never met her, but I'm told she spoke to my Scottish grandpa with a German accent. One of the only photos I have of Emma shows a beautiful young woman with a high, embroidered collar, looking very prim and pious.

Her songbook is also a prayer book and contains the Augsburg Confession—in German, of course. I wonder what Emma would think of the continual squabbles among the "reformed" and their splintered denominations. I think she would find some comfort in ecumenical coalitions, but I sense she might be disappointed, as I have been, at the divisions over dogmas, doctrines, and distracting trivialities.

There are few Luthers left (Martin Luther King was one). Few dare to risk being outed as heretics by posting honest, disturbing truth. Perhaps it's more comfortable to look back to honor reformers than do some serious reforming in our day.

Twenty-eight
No Secular Crusades

My own religious history has many chapters. As I thumb back through the pages there is a jumble of joys and heartaches as well as sweet and bittersweet memories. When I recall one incident, another pops up — it seems an endless thread of images and stories that keep me wondering why and what was I thinking, and why.

Before his death in February, 2018, Billy Graham's short syndicated column appeared in the *Citizen-Times* near my "Highland Views" column. I often scanned his piece, and I was never surprised at his "biblical answer" and call to Christ. His reply to a reader's question about people turning to secular worldviews instead of faith caught my attention, and it seemed important to assure readers there is no crusade for nonbelief — yet. Should there be?

I was once "there." Now I'm "here." I'm speaking of the small bubble called fundamentalism, where the world is a very scary, dangerous, threatening thing. I was a fundamental believer, then an evangelical, then pentecostal, then conservative, then liberal Christian. Then ... well ... here I am.

Once upon a time I was "saved" by Billy Graham. He would be quick to correct me — God saved me when I "asked Jesus into my heart." Okay. But it was through a "crusade" that I heard the preaching and "accepted Jesus" into my life. I was only thirteen, but apparently so lost, already such a desperately sinful human being, that the Lord of the Universe had to kill his only Son for ME. I felt terrible, and terribly afraid. God was angry at my sin but loved me so much he had His only child—once a teen like me—executed so He could forgive me. For the next forty years or so I was a believer, following Jesus through high school, college, seminary, and years of ministry.

So when Rev. Graham was asked about the rise of secularism—why, according to some polls, more people are drifting from religious faith—his response was not surprising, but his "biblically-based" answer seemed to invite (or at least elicit) a clear response, since I'm one of those dreaded seculars. Now and then I think it wise, perhaps necessary, to respond to the fears and fantasies that drive some to hate nonbelievers so much.

Rev. Graham's first comment to the questioner was, "The poll you mention may well be correct; similar surveys seem to point in the same direction. We are living in an increasingly secular and non-religious society, and many people today never think about God or make Him a part of their lives."

He's right, of course. Increasing numbers of people are leaving churches, synagogues, mosques, temples and sometimes even faith itself. Yet a lot of people still believe something: maybe they consider themselves "spiritual" or have a vague idea of a "creative force" in the universe. There is a wide spectrum of belief. And yes, a lot of others choose to not believe in the supernatural any longer. As Billy wrote, they may never think about God—at least the Christian God.

Why are people choosing not to believe? Billy's

answer was, "One reason is because we have failed to pass on our faith in Christ to the next generation ... we have failed to explain the Gospel to them and urge them to commit their lives to Christ." People aren't becoming believers because believers aren't doing their job. This is the old missionary zeal that causes believers to feel guilt for not converting more of the world to keep people from divine punishment. That's a huge burden to bear.

He acknowledged that Christians need to show more love; however, he added, "There are ... other reasons why our world seems to be less and less religious. Growing materialism, a preoccupation with pleasure, pressures from a secular media, the lessening of family ties, growing immorality — the list is almost endless."

This was Rev. Graham's message throughout his long life (he died at 99.) He warned that secular people only want more and more pleasure, seeking to destroy families and offering nothing but ungodly materialism and immorality. Pretty bad. "The list is almost endless." Very black and white. Note the danger of the "secular media" — the whispers of satan?

He ended his warnings, as he had when I heard him all those years ago: "Only Christ can satisfy the deepest longings of the human heart, and only He can change our lives and give us hope for the future."

It's a simple message. Almost irresistible. But millions are now resisting, because millions have seen that believing in one god or another is no guarantee someone will be good, honest, moral, loving, or happy. As the world has gotten smaller and people more interconnected, we find there's more than just one faith to choose from, and being humanist, agnostic, atheist, or a freethinker can be a reasonable alternative.

At around the same time as Billy Graham's column appeared, the newspaper ran a story about people setting up tables along some of our hiking trails to proselytize. I was not surprised. Back in my evangelistic days I would hand Bibles and booklets to anyone, anywhere, anytime. There was no time to listen—it was my job to save them! Now I find it very sad. Preaching about other worlds when this one—with all of its problems—is so wonderful and beautiful and there's so much to learn from so many interesting people.

Believe it or not there is no "secular crusade." But sometimes I think: maybe there should be.

Twenty-nine
"Blessed Are the Poor"? That Can't Be Right

It can be helpful to have a rather strange vocational path. Before religious work I was a special education instructor for six years. I could mine that field for a long time for stories. Then, through my career as a chaplain, I was with and among the poorest folks on a daily basis. Going on to work with at-risk youth, gardening and building trails on a northwest island, then running a shelter before managing homes for lower-income seniors ... there are tales to tell.

Is there a thread that ties the tales together? If there is it may be a consistent interest in what people on the margins of our communities are experiencing and what they have to teach more privileged folks like me. Another interwoven thread would be the faith response to these neighbors who have very little material wealth but a great deal of wisdom to share, if we care to listen.

Patty had Down syndrome and was often in the "community living skills" class I taught at a residential school for people with mental and physical disabilities. She liked to giggle and tease. She also had a temper and could stomp her feet and yell. Even though we couldn't always understand what she was saying, her feelings were loud and clear.

Patty liked to wear lots of costume jewelry, and she always carried a small purse with just about everything she valued tucked inside. No one, including the teacher, was ever allowed to touch that bright-colored purse.

Patty, like most of the rest of my students, had very little to call her own. But she was content with what she had, even if she loved to shop and find other small things to stuff in her bag.

"Blessed are the poor."

John dropped his heavy rucksack on the floor and sat down with a heavy sigh. His camp had been washed out again, and everything he valued was stuffed into that small pack. I poured him a hot cup of coffee and gave him a fresh blanket and a new sleeping bag just donated by the synagogue. John's gratefulness needed no words, but he thanked me anyway. He smiled when I brushed it off. "I'm only giving what has been given to give," I said, or something like that.

A few months later, after John was found dead in a bathroom at the mall, our chaplaincy team drew together a small circle in the park to remember him. Knowing that John was Scottish, we read from the poet Robert Burns and a passage from John's Bible, which I retrieved from the shambles of his tent on the hillside.

Burns wrote: "So in lone Poverty's dominion drear, sits meek Content with light, unanxious heart; Welcomes the rapid moments, bids them part; Nor asks if they bring [anything] to hope or fear."

John was very anxious sometimes. Where would he safely sleep tonight? Where could he hide today from the fearful, judging eyes and the prowling police? Yet there was a certain contentment in his eyes, a sparkle of hope, and he impressed us with his gentleness.

"Blessed are the poor."

Some tell us "blessed" means being happy, as if people who have little should be happy with what they

have, not ask us for handouts, and stay in their place —
even if that's hell. Others tell us Luke had it wrong (6:20)
and Matthew got it right (5:3): Blessed are the poor *in
spirit*. It has to mean this is a spiritual thing, not literally
referring to those with few possessions.

We hear more and more about the "prosperity
gospel" and those "blessed" by God with success.
They fervently pray to have a large home full of "God's
abundance." For some, that proves the Lord is watching
over them, pleased to surround them with "divine gifts."
That makes them happy and makes God happy too. But,
are we ever satisfied? Do we ever have "enough"?

We've turned it around and upside down. The new
"improved" gospel proclaims: "Blessed are those with
much, for God has blessed them."

I sometimes think back to those long ago days when
our circle of youthful believers yearned for the end, the
Second Coming, the "rapture" up into heaven. We were
only young people with the promise of life ahead of us,
but we watched the skies for any sign of "His return."
We were His children and He was coming back for
us — to take us Home to be with Him forever. We knew
without a doubt, it would all happen very soon.

Well, it didn't. We didn't have time to be disappointed
because, it might be today!

"Blessed are the poor … for theirs is the kingdom of
heaven."

It never occurred to our youthful minds — and none
of our revered Bible teachers ever suggested — that
this verse might be about someone else. As I like to
say, what if people really took the "Word at its word"
and believed it? What if Jesus was literally saying the

kingdom belongs to poor folks—poverty is the key to open heaven's door?

Voices rise in protest: "Heavens! He surely didn't mean to say poor people would be taken to heaven first—before any of the 'true believers'! What good is faith, if we aren't the first to enter the heavenly gates! Obviously He means to bless poor 'Christians.' Besides, people are poor for many reasons (usually their fault) and they may not even believe in God. How can we make sense of this?"

Patty, John and countless others are ready to teach—maybe "bless" us—if we have the ears to hear and eyes to see.

Thirty
Ingersoll: His Middle Name was Green

As a freethinking writer it's a great delight to expose readers to great minds in the history of Freethought like Robert Green Ingersoll. His liberty of mind, educated by nature, made him a significant voice of common sense, more needed today than ever.

Like many abolitionists and women's rights advocates such as Elizabeth Cady Stanton, Robert Green Ingersoll emerged (converted?) from a religious household. He was not anti-religion but pro-reason. Though he is largely forgotten today, his voice of reason and humanity — sprinkled with humor — still echoes.

Like some modern comedians (George Carlin, Stephen Colbert, Samantha Bee), Ingersoll made people of faith laugh at themselves, and caused believers and nonbelievers alike to consider growing "as great as the continent."

A magnificent orator, Ingersoll (1833-1899), was asked to speak in Peoria, Illinois on July 4, 1876 — the 100th anniversary of the Declaration of Independence. We would do well to remember his liberating words on that historic day.

Though he was born in Dresden, New York, Ingersoll was well known in Illinois, since he worked as a lawyer in Peoria and other cities. He had also served as a Union colonel in the Civil War. His father, an abolitionist preacher, was unwelcome in many towns. By the 1870s, Robert was already "famously infamous" as a kind of Freethought evangelist. People called him "The Great Agnostic" for his entertaining manner of dismantling religious orthodoxy with incisive wit and humor that would draw crowds of the faithful and faithless to his lectures.

He began his centennial speech by proclaiming that, "The Declaration of Independence is the grandest, the bravest, and the profoundest political document that was ever signed by the representatives of a people ... the embodiment of physical and moral courage and of political wisdom." As his crescendo built, he proclaimed, "With one blow, with one stroke of the pen, they struck down all the cruel, heartless barriers that aristocracy, that priestcraft, that kingcraft had raised between man and man." We can imagine the audience was stirred by this imagery. The Founders fired the first shot of revolution with a pen!

Notice how he says independence concerns "heartless barriers" between people. Not only "kingcraft" but aristocracy and "priestcraft" can build those barriers. Ingersoll's hero Thomas Paine (a neglected Founder) crafted his own arguments for social as well as individual independence including freedom to choose what to think and believe. Both of these revolutionary thinkers had strong words for kings, whether sitting on earthly or heavenly thrones. Now you can guess why Paine and Ingersoll are often forgotten.

Imagine if Ingersoll's speech went viral on Instagram or YouTube. The good colonel was firing his own shot across the bow of irrational religion. From the reports of his lectures, his crowds were enthusiastic; even when some disagreed, there was frequent applause and great laughter. No brawls; no riots: this was entertainment, but with a strong sense that honest truth was being told, as uncomfortable as that can be.

What I find consistently intriguing with Ingersoll is the appeal to Reason, Humanity, and Nature. The gift of secularism and its "infidel preachers" like Ingersoll is its grounding in naturalistic thought. This is pretty simple to understand. Natural reasoning, rather than a super-natural source, is the origin of wisdom. Nature is down-to-earth—as near as the brain, the mind, the body. Any other "authority" out there, an authority that is not evidenced in the natural world, that we can not see and hear and touch, has to be open to question. This is the heart of what "freedom" and "independence" means.

Think of it this way: someone claims his faith allows him to treat someone else unfairly. Naturalistic thought responds, How is that ethical? Someone claims her religion should be given special treatment. Naturalistic thought asks, Why yours?

Common sense rules; reason schools.

When nature and naturalistic thought are the basis of our lives, wonderful (even revolutionary) things can happen—like new forms of independent thinking and living. What Lincoln said about our national origins can be applied to our daily lives: "conceived in liberty and dedicated to the proposition that all are created equal."

Ingersoll's voice rang clear: "It has been a favorite idea with me that our forefathers were educated by Nature, that they grew grand as the continent upon which they landed; that the great rivers—the wide plains—the splendid lakes—the lonely forests—the sublime mountains—that all these things stole into and became a part of their being, and they grew great as the country in which they lived."

What is the great idea, the grand plan, to emerge from this radical (rooted) way of thinking? Something rare yet beautiful: interconnected relationships, educated by nature.

Ingersoll proclaims: "They had the idea—the Puritans, the Catholics, the Episcopalians, the Baptists, the Quakers, and a few Freethinkers ... that they would like to form a new nation." When we're called back to this cooperative liberty, it doesn't matter if we believe or don't believe. We all become more natural and reasonable (hopefully); we make a choice to practice E Pluribus Unum and become a little more free and a bit "greener."

Robert Green Ingersoll listened to Nature, let it steal into him, and then courageously spoke truth. We could use more of that.

Craggy Gardens in the Sky, Blue Ridge Parkway, Asheville NC

Thirty-one
The Face of Nature

Anthropomorphism. A very important word for understanding religion "in the image of humanity." We put our human face on just about everything, sometimes to make sense of our world, and sometimes to worship our own reflection. That's a disturbing thought for many people of faith, yet it's hard to get around it. We make our gods in our own image.

Nature suffers when we do that. True, a "sacred grove" of trees may be preserved or a "holy river" may be recognized for its "spiritual power," but what happens when thousands or millions of pilgrims walk over those roots or bathe in those waters?

The trail out of "god-making" can be long and arduous but ultimately liberating. When Nature no longer has our face, we can truly "face" the world as a wild place we still don't understand very well at all.

Carol and I drove the length of the Blue Ridge Parkway from Waynesboro, Virginia to Asheville, NC. We've done more of the Parkway here, but haven't quite completed the whole 469-mile "Belt of Beauty." It's an amazement at every turn with vistas that will leave you speechless.

At a trailhead in Virginia we met an elderly couple from the north of England who had driven all the way from New Orleans. They suggested we stop at a country store further south at Meadows of Dan. We stopped by the market and were immediately aware of something unusual. As we wandered the aisles of jams and hams, nooks and books, we found ourselves singing along with the music playing on the store PA system. It was all "sacred" music, catchy old tunes about faith and Jesus.

Humming and singing all the songs among the shoppers and shelves, I was smiling, aware that some might think I was a faithful churchgoing believer.

Hearing these old tunes brought back youth group and camp songs like "Turn Your Eyes upon Jesus":

"Look full in His wonderful face; and the things of earth will grow strangely dim, in the light of His glory and grace."

We would weep as we strummed our cheap guitars, gazing up to heaven.

Music is a powerful way to turn and shape our emotions and beliefs. Like the Parkway, music takes us to the heights and depths—to mountains and hollers of feeling.

What I wonder about sometimes is how much we allow melodies and lyrics to sink into our minds and color the world around us. I think of those songs and the message they tell of sin and sorrow and salvation. I can appreciate the melodies and don't mind singing along, sometimes. Yet I feel some concern that many don't realize the questionable theologies that get buried in your brain.

We sang earnestly of a face so bright it would cause "the things of earth" to "grow strangely dim" (a kind of spiritual eclipse). As the verse in Isaiah says, "The grass withers, the flower fades" because the glorious presence above outshines it all. What does this say about valuing our life here or caring for our world?

There are those on the other end of the spiritual spectrum who see the "face of God" everywhere in all things. For these folks (sometimes calling themselves Pantheists), looking into the eyes of Nature is gazing into the face of God (gods or goddesses). This is a pagan way of viewing the world, and since "pagan" simply means a person of the wild and open countryside I would guess many of us are secret pagans—or at least sense that "land and lord" are not far apart.

Though most Christian theologies reject this notion of God in Nature, many people experience "spirituality" in the natural world. They feel closer to the "divine" nearer to the "sacred" earth. What does this language suggest?

This leads back to my main concern. The more we are seeking a "presence" or "spirit" in nature, the more we seem to lose the immediate (un-mediated) experience of nature's endlessly wonderful lessons. We'd rather listen to preachers and scriptures than to park naturalists and scientists—to hear church music rather than bird music. We become distracted by our beliefs about the world, particularly other worlds. As I see it, we lose the goodness of nature when we look beyond it toward something or Someone above or behind it. We overlook the "face value" of nature.

When the earth fades and grows "strangely dim," this can lead to not caring what happens to the natural environment—our home. As they say, some people are "so heavenly minded they're no earthly good." Why support efforts to conserve and preserve wild areas or protect wildlife when it's all "passing away" and the incredible beauty around us is "just a distraction" from "living for God" and preparing for heaven? This mentality can have serious consequences.

I once felt that Nature was God—that the world was, in a sense, God incarnate. In ministry, it was people, human beings, who could embody the divine. When I cleared trails in the Pacific Northwest, I felt I was coming closer to the "Spirit of Nature" (I even wrote a song about that). Then I realized what I was doing. I was denigrating, you might say desecrating, the world all around me by spiritualizing it. I stopped in my tracks, literally, and let go of a "spiritual" way of seeing the world. That felt natural.

When our world no longer has the "face of God" or speaks with the "voice of God" there can be meaningful music too—singing of Nature as nature, for itself and itself alone.

Thirty-two
What Does It Mean To Be a Religious Progressive?

I peruse several websites for insight and enlightenment about other former — and some still current — believers. A blog by a pastor who calls himself a "Christian Naturalist and Secular Humanist" briefly made my head spin, but I read more of his thought and wrote to say I understood, though I could never refer to myself in that way. Anything goes in religious labeling these days; I understand that, too. When you're no longer in the orthodox camp resting in the tents of theology, tied down with creeds — well, what do *you call yourself?*

There were times during my chaplain years that people were being told to avoid me for one reason or another. One man was spreading the word on the street that I was getting rich off being a chaplain. Thankfully, most knew that was untrue. Another person spread the rumor that I wasn't a Christian. It was not true then, but had some truth in it.

It's hard to find a "true Christian." That is, everyone can be suspected by anyone else of not being a "true" this or that. One group says followers of another group are not "true believers." One faction interprets their holy book in one way, and says other interpretations are "in error." When this gets really ugly, "judge not lest ye be judged" is thrown out completely, and we have a regular judge-fest with epic scripture battles that no one wins.

Growing up in the church and studying the Bible for

years, I chose to enter seminary and go on into ministry. Along the way I came to see that being a "true believer" was actually about practicing a "true way of living" based on honesty and compassion toward others. What are creeds while someone bleeds?

During those years, I didn't hear the word "progressive" much. "Progress" to a faithful follower meant moving toward deeper understanding of others — and of what was most needed in a troubled world. Emerging from seminary, some of us felt inspired by radical "Liberation" movements, particularly actions in Latin America often led by Catholic priests; in that context, progress meant concern for people suffering oppression or injustice as well as confronting restrictive forms of thinking. It was a matter of both mind and body. "Community" meant including people in poverty, but more than that, stepping aside so they could be the leaders. The most ignored voices among us may have the "good news" we most need to hear. As we saw it, this was being a "true follower of the Great Liberator — Jesus."

Here's the thing. In my mind it's pretty much meaningless to hear folks argue over who is a "true believer" in this or that faith. As great thinkers have taught, the point is action, not labels. I go one step further and say that theology is too much of a distraction from what needs to be done, so I am a critic of too much "God-talk."

I recently struck up a conversation with a former colleague who calls himself a "Progressive Christian." I've been asking him some questions and he's been kind enough to engage in some friendly dialogue.

He says the heart of the Christian worldview and message is "mysticism." I've been eager for more explanation of that, since he also says he does not believe in the supernatural. This has me raising eyebrows and face-palming.

I understand his point, that there is a thread throughout church history of individuals who felt that God and the Universe were somehow One. An intimate relationship with the "divine" causes some to saturate the material world with the "spiritual." A class I once taught on mystics included Christian, Jewish, Sufi, Buddhist, Hindu, and Native American voices. Many of their thoughts seemed very close to Paganism, a deep stream of thought underlying many religions. Yet, none of them ever dismissed the supernatural. For a "religion," that would make no sense.

My former colleague says some branches of modern science affirm this sense of interrelation. Perhaps. But why use ancient words from spiritual traditions to explain that? Science is awfully wonderful at expressing the awesome wonder of it all without using "snowflake words" (like "spirit" or "sacred") that melt when I try to hold them in my brain.

I keep wondering: What does any of this mean? Practically speaking, how can a reasoning person make sense of it? Perhaps it's beyond reason? If so, how can we communicate meaningfully? Calling oneself a mystic or a progressive in matters of faith sounds good, but if one has a "connection to the Universe," why label that with one religion or one God?

I need "progressive" believers to help me understand a little more. Is there a "super-natural," and if so, how would we know that? If God equals Nature, why use the name "God" or claim one faith instead of another? Isn't this simply the old "anthropomorphism"—making God in our own image? And, how does one "pray" to Nature or "worship" the Universe?

It's clear, I have many lingering questions. I guess that's one reason people warned their friends about me all those years ago. At least now I'm making some progress ... I think.

Thirty-three
The Interfaith Alternative

Creating connections between various faiths by inviting representatives to innovative events comes naturally to me as well as to my wife. Finding the boundary points that divide this group from that group and then looking for ways to identify or build openings or bridges is the challenge: it can be quite delightful, and sometimes frustrating.

When secular voices are included in that mix, interesting things can happen. I joined a theology professor in leading a retreat on sacredness in nature. During one Q&A session, one participant, a Dominican Sister, asked me, with distress in her voice, "You aren't an atheist, are you?!" I tried to calm her alarm. Since I've known and respected her for years, I could gently explain that I have no more theological views of the world, only natural. The fact that we could discuss our views in a room full of believers from various traditions, was refreshing. Later, the Sister gave me a hug and kiss on the cheek.

In 2016 we were driving across the country, state by state, crossing rivers, mountain ranges, and expansive open spaces. Apart from the natural beauty, we looked for those "Welcome" signs at the borders of each state. Wherever we stopped to rest or to enjoy the beauty, people were our countrymen and women. We usually didn't think, "This is a Montanan" or "That's a Kansan." We could both appreciate the differences and the similarities. Americans were Americans. People are people.

Carol and I were involved in interfaith work for many

years. We were building networks of congregations and nonprofits across borders of belief, hanging out welcome signs for groups often excluded, like seculars and minority traditions.

Inter-religious efforts have grown in popularity over the last century. Since the first World Parliament of Religions was convened in Chicago in 1893, interfaith cooperation has grown from just getting people in the room, to deeper dialogues and collaborative coalitions. Today, multi-faith organizations, such as Interfaith Youth Core, North American Interfaith Network, and United Religions Initiative, sometimes include secular voices and leadership.

I asked Vicki Garlock, Nurture Coordinator and Curriculum Developer at Asheville's Jubilee! Community congregation and a facilitator of Asheville Interfaith, to respond to a few questions.

Asked how her faith tradition views nonbelievers, Vicki replied, "Jubilee! is a fully independent, 'progressive-type' Christian church. We have no idea" what members believe.

I find that quite refreshing. She told me that one of her kids is drawn to Native American practices and another is an atheist. Young people in her congregation have many beliefs, from Sufi to evangelical.

I asked her if the church has any interest in changing the minds of nonbelievers.

"Not at all. Since we do not profess any given creed at Jubilee! it's not clear what our conversion goals would be! We place a premium on people ... in the world at large."

Regarding secular worldviews, she replied, "I suspect most "Jubilants," including the kids in our program, view those with secular worldviews as yet another important piece in the rich tapestry of human life on this planet. At Jubilee! we try to move beyond simple tolerance of and co-existence with those who hold different views; we try to express and live into the idea of deep appreciation for what all sentient beings bring to our community and our world." That seems very open and welcoming.

Regarding the balance between naturalistic and supernatural beliefs, Vicki said, "Nature is an important piece of what we do at Jubilee! both with the adults and with the kids. Our themes change quarterly with the solstices/equinoxes; we sometimes celebrate neo-Pagan [holy days], like Brigid and Samhain; and we sometimes honor secular earth-based holidays, like Earth Day and World Water Day. We also have an Earth Team at Jubilee! that offers opportunities to commune with nature and/or to work toward sustainable living. All these things help connect us to the earth and remind us of our place in the web of living beings."

In response to my usual question about dialogue, she replied, "Jubilee! is firmly committed to honest and compassionate dialogue with people of all faiths or no faith. We honor rituals from other faith traditions, we read from the sacred texts of other traditions, and we count people from a variety of belief systems not just as friends, but as parishioners." She added that their kids' program offers "opportunities to explore topics from a no-faith perspective, including our themes of Peace, Awe & Wonder, Compassion, and Embracing the Darkness." They also "make a point to present the creation narratives given to us by science, including the

Big Bang Theory and Evolution." You don't hear that too often from faith communities.

Beyond this, Vicki says that "because we are a church, what is experienced on Sunday mornings and what we offer to the kids is generally grounded in the faith-based traditions of the world [rather than a secular perspective]." That makes good sense.

She said that "as questions arise" she's happy to engage in conversation with nonbelievers.

I find it encouraging that a faith-centered community here in Asheville seems so open to listening rather than preaching. I have yet to visit Vicki's church, but I'm guessing a person like me could feel included.

Gathering a wide collection of worldviews takes some risk. Bringing people of many faiths and no faiths together to build relationships, working and celebrating alongside each other, has challenges. But it seems worth it because — what's the alternative? The same old fenced and defended religion.

We could use more journeys across the borders of faith, don't you think?

Thirty-four
Seeing through Stevie Wonder's Eyes

I really love those moments when a famous person speaks out on some issue and we all nod and applaud in approval—until they finish. We aren't prepared for the zinger when we gasp or groan, "Why did they have to say that?!" This is particularly smile-producing for me when someone like Stevie Wonder says some very spiritual things that many believers like to hear, but then he adds something a little too inclusive and open. People find it's not just about them, but they have to think of others and other views, feelings, beliefs. That can be hard to swallow.

Truth-tellers don't really care if people can swallow and digest what they serve up. And often they don't care what people say because they are simply expressing their personal perspective. It just happens to be true.

Superstar musician Stevie Wonder was interviewed on NPR (August 30, 2017) and said some remarkable things.

"I think that my thing is basically, God—when I think about it, I say, 'God, how can I make you even more happy?' Because, you know, obviously I'm appreciative of the fans and success and all that. But to please God is my greatest joy."

I would imagine most Christians would be fine with that. But "Mr. Wonder" goes on:

"And for those who might be Muslim, to please the

God that you serve, Allah, or whatever your religion is. Like I said before, it's not about the religion, it's about the relationship."

He's not finished.

"And so my thing right now is I'm thinking: How can we deal with this situation where people are prostituting the most high with their negativity, with their evil? That hurts my heart so deeply. And that's everywhere. And so, to me, the one thing you've heard through and through every religion is: Hey, just love ... That's the most important thing: Just love. That's what's gonna see us through. So when I hear these little children singing my songs or singing songs, hearing those voices and I think of those little kids in Manchester, just going to see a concert and then someone uses that as a source of their anger—it's unacceptable. I don't care who you are or where you're from, it doesn't matter. And for me, not seeing anybody, it means that I'm looking at their souls."

This amazing artist who's sold something like 100 million records and earned 25 Grammy awards, has earned the right to use his piano pulpit for a truth-telling sermon. The young people who were killed in the concert in Manchester were there only to find joy in singing. Stevie has the "eyes to see" the shadow side of any faith that would harm innocents.

But how is this "prostituting the most high with their negativity"? Though he says that the "one thing" we've heard from every religion is "just love," he also understands there are angry people, even angry people with faith—an angry faith—who choose to harm others by using their god to force their negative feelings on others. Judging others and hurting others to prove that your "God of Love" is best and your faith is the only way is a form of prostitution.

In the Bible we find an embarrassing story — one of those unmentionable passages no one dares to preach — when God tells the prophet Hosea to "Go, take for yourself a wife of whoredom and have children" (Hosea 1). Why would God demand such an outrageous thing? A lesson of course. "The land prostitutes itself by forsaking the Lord." Hosea's "wife" (purchased for some silver, a loaf of bread, and a bottle of wine) is forced to have three children, each given a name to show God's displeasure. There are other "spiritual instructions" in the Book of Hosea, but it seems to be an ancient affirmation of Stevie Wonder's observation: there are angry people who, in the name of an angry God, take out their anger on others.

What did this unnamed woman think about being used as a "divine lesson"? A poor woman is bought and sold because a man is told to make a lesson out of her since his God feels cheated on by his adulterous people.

I think we can guess why this story isn't taught in Sunday School. Bible experts will tell us the "message" is more important than the details, yet a human being, the woman, is one detail we can't ignore.

Why spend so much time on this terrible story? Because, as Stevie says, using another person to display your own negativity and anger is "unacceptable." As he says, "For me, not seeing anybody, it means that I'm looking at their souls."

A secular person might not speak of looking at "souls," but we can all choose to "see" — to consider real human persons.

Years ago I remember how much I enjoyed the album, *Songs in the Key of Life*. One song was quite beautiful, almost haunting: "Love's in Need of Love Today."

> Love's in need of love today;
> Don't delay, send yours in right away;
> Hate's goin' 'round, breaking many hearts;
> Stop it please, before it's gone too far.
> The force of evil plans to make you its possession,
> and it will if we let it destroy everybody.
> We all must take precautionary measures;
> if love and peace you treasure,
> then you'll hear me when I say:
> Love's in need of love today.

If only more of our world could see like Stevie, and sing along.

Thirty-five
Thoreau, Darwin, and Nature's Book

July 12, 2017, was the 200th birthday of Henry David Thoreau. To honor the saunterer of Walden Pond on his bicentennial, I found it inspiring to evoke Thoreau's theme of nature as an open book while connecting him with his English counterpart, Charles Darwin, who shared a delight in discoveries near and far.

Ever since I first read Henry Thoreau in my evangelical college, I've been drawn to his character and craft. With his philosophical mind and deep curiosity immersing him in the natural environment, Henry was up to his head in the wild woods and up to his heart in love for nature.

Not long ago I asked a neighbor why he was the only one in his family to leave the faith. With a smile he casually replied, "Books." I understood exactly what he meant. The wider our reading, the more viewpoints we are exposed to and the better able we are to weigh our choices and make our own informed decisions.

One such thought-provoking book, Randall Fuller's *The Book That Changed America*, tells the story of the first copy of *On the Origin of Species* to arrive in America. A small group of thinkers gathered in Concord, Massachusetts in 1860 to pass around Charles Darwin's revolutionary book, and it had a profound effect on their lives. Each was active in abolition, and the new book inspired their radical work. You could say their thinking "evolved."

Henry Thoreau was one of that Concord circle, and naturally I was especially interested in his response to "Origin." As Fuller puts it, "Darwin's portrait of a teeming, pulsating natural world deeply resonated with Thoreau. [The book] revealed nature as process, as continual becoming ... Reading the 'Origin,' Thoreau discovered someone else who understood nature as he did: abounding and vibrant, each niche swarming, each [space] filled with life, each living thing a small part of constant change...." Henry was only a bit over 40 when he found this amazing book, and he could barely put it down. The impact was not so much the theory of natural selection but the wonderful affirmation of life's great diversity.

Darwin himself was delighted to find evidence that "all the forms of life, ancient and recent, make together one grand system: for all are connected by generation." Thoreau must have shared that delight because, like Darwin, his study of nature affirmed the words at the conclusion of "Origin": "There is grandeur in this view of life ... from so simple a beginning endless forms most beautiful and most wonderful have been, and are being, evolved."

It strikes me as strange, and frankly irritating, that Darwin and his theories are met with such fearful resistance even today. Darwin himself believed in a creative force of some kind: he was not at all against religion or trying to remove God from the story of life. Yet, he was willing to go where the facts would take him. If those facts cause people to question or alter their inherited beliefs, so be it.

As Fuller points out, Darwin left theology to study

nature, just as another American contemporary, Ralph Waldo Emerson, did. That doesn't mean they didn't have any faith — they were just more interested in reasonable explanations of the way the world works rather than theories of how another world may work. Fuller explains that for Thoreau, "The world ... is rich with mystery — just not the kind that religious tradition has led people to expect and rely upon." We may have to "abandon old faiths and old patterns of belief ... while searching for knowledge and insight...."

Thoreau died in 1862 at the young age of 44. Even in his last months, he was, in Fuller's words, on a "pilgrimage to know the world." He incessantly jotted notes in his journal, keeping track of his own tracks through nature's classroom.

Two centuries after his birth, I think Henry deserves to be honored for his writing, but mostly for his independent mind. He should be remembered, like Darwin, as an honest explorer.

I suggest re-reading *Walden* or selections from his *Journal* or his essays on *Walking* or *Civil Disobedience*, keeping in mind this young thinker was not just "in his head" — he was a scientist, an activist, and a flute player.

When I visited the Old Manse — the Emerson and Hawthorne home in Concord — a few years ago, a docent led us through the house, into the room where Emerson wrote his first book, *Nature* (1836). She pointed to the small collapsible desk on one wall and said it was believed that Thoreau built it. As we were leaving I noticed the wooden support holding the desktop was about to slip down, which I imagined would shatter the old desk. I approached the docent, who said no one was supposed to touch things, but she gave me permission to readjust the support. I felt I was not only doing a small part to preserve the historical significance of that small desk; I was touching something Henry had touched.

Then again, whenever we touch nature, Henry and Charles are pretty close by.

Thirty-six
The Wisdom of Doubt

Studying Philosophy in a Christian university, I loved the intellectual stimulation and welcomed the wisdom of any wise voice regardless of belief. Emerging from narrow-mindedness and a protected worldview, it was truly liberating to hear other voices that confronted complacency with honest, incisive questions. Questions became my friends, and I learned not to fear them but to practice consistent self-reflection and an impatience with easy and often irrational "answers."

The poet Jim Gronvold is a personal friend. After years as a nonprofit leader, he is now retired and has time to write. His 2017 collection of poetry, *Star Thistle*, includes this little gem I read to a class I was teaching:

> Knowing the need
> to understand
> what it all
> is all about,
>
> I also know
> the freedom
> of not needing
> to figure it out,
>
> of feeling enough
> uncertainty
> to value the
> wisdom of doubt.

The truth of this verse sticks and pricks like a thistle. The "need to understand" has a strong pull. Our curiosity and wonder push us to want to know more. Yet, as the poet reminds us, there is freedom in "not needing to figure it out," a freedom in uncertainty that brings us "to value the wisdom of doubt." An important lesson.

I was taught as a youngster not to doubt. Asking polite questions was fine, but you should never, ever doubt God, the Bible, the teachings of the church, or the pastor. I learned that "the one who doubts is like a wave of the sea," because a doubter is "double-minded and unstable" and shouldn't expect to receive anything from the Lord. [James 1: 5-8]

As I studied this more deeply I discovered there are two kinds of wisdom: from "above" (dropping down from the divine) and "earthly" (from below; devilish). I learned that God is the only one to give wisdom, so just have faith, and never doubt. This was affirmed by Jesus, who told his disciples to "have faith and do not doubt" because "whatever you ask for in prayer with faith, you will receive." [Matthew 21: 21-22]

Even as a child I think I secretly doubted that. "Whatever I ask" I will get? Friends and family got sick, had accidents, died. My prayers weren't answered then. I guess I just didn't have enough faith. I suppose believers have come to this conclusion for many centuries. Who has "enough faith" anyway? You don't see many people throwing mountains into the sea.

In my eye-opening college years when I began to emerge from believing in one god, one faith, one church to a wider view of the world, I was doubting heavily. At that time I wasn't doubting that there was a god, but questioning if the god I was taught was the "real" or only god. As a philosophy major with a minor in religion, studying at an evangelical college, I discovered there were many understandings of god and faith. I found there were many good people who doubted too, and it didn't make them bad people. I also saw there were millions of people doing good things in the name of different gods, or in the name of good, and the world was a better place for all of us. Though some warned me I shouldn't study philosophy because I would be led into doubt, I came to value the philosophical path, practicing the love of wisdom as a way to creatively question without fear. I'm grateful for my professors who were people of fearless faith.

Maybe we've been misled a little. Maybe a lot. Sometimes, with the best of intentions, teachers and preachers have told us there is a special wisdom only available from one faith, one book. These specially chosen, exceptionally wise teachers might even tell us not to doubt their exceptional wisdom. Using verses from James and Jesus, they also claim Paul was right when he warned believers: "Do not deceive yourselves. If you think that you are wise in this age, you should become fools so that you may become wise." Then comes the zinger: "For the wisdom of this world [a secular, non-biblical worldview] is foolishness with God." [First Corinthians 3: 18-19] Makes us wonder: Who's being fooled?

"Esoteric" means specialized knowledge understood by only a few. That isn't bad or dangerous in itself, but we can see how easy it would be to manipulate the message — and, in the wrong hands, control people too. The ironic twist is that it takes some wisdom to see that.

Perhaps, next to philosophers and scientists, the poets

are the best ones to help us in our search for knowledge and wisdom. At least they seem to understand that words are slippery and misunderstanding leads to misuse of words. In other words, words are important and powerful, and need to be examined for truth and wisdom. With faith or without faith, we can feel free to fearlessly examine.

Is it such a bad thing to toss around thoughts, ideas and beliefs like waves or wind? Should we ever hesitate to wisely wonder and ask the hard questions?

I doubt it.

Thirty-seven
Fostering Contemplation

As a secular person who is still interested in conversations and relationships with people of faith, approaching religious leaders comes naturally to me. Since I was an ordained person for many years, I'm not at all put off or intimidated by clergy – in fact, I'm very aware of the human person behind the "revered" titles, garb, and respected positions.

Previously, Muslim and Jewish leaders have responded to questions relating to their thoughts on secular people (agnostics, atheists, freethinkers). I also had a conversation with the Rev. Jerry Prickett of St. Matthias Episcopal Church in Asheville. The church has an interesting history as the first African American congregation in Asheville.

I asked him how his faith tradition views nonbelievers. He responded:

"The baptismal covenant of the Episcopal Church ends with two questions that speak to this: 'Will you seek and serve Christ in all persons, loving your neighbor as yourself?' 'Will you strive for justice and peace among all people, and respect the dignity of every human being?' Jesus, in his parable of the Good Samaritan, identifies everybody as our neighbor. The Episcopal Church was among the early groups seeking justice and peace and dignity of all. Scripture, reason, and tradition are the guiding elements for the Church. All three have influenced the approach that Episcopalians have taken toward justice and peace initiatives taken since the late 1700s."

I'm struck by how the Rev. Prickett places the approach to nonbelievers in a wide historical context from the time of Jesus through the traditions and covenants of the church. The emphasis on peace, justice, and dignity has historically been a central concern for the secular community as well.

When I asked him how important it is to change the minds of nonbelievers, to persuade people toward his faith, he replied, "We are not inclined to proselytize on street corners or in conversations with those who express a lack of faith. Though we may not initiate the conversation about faith, we talk about it in positive terms that, we hope, fosters contemplation."

This has been my delightful experience over the years working with Episcopalians. There has been a strong sense of grounding in their churches while bringing an openness to learn and engage in dialogue as they are active in the greater community. During my years as a chaplain, I served alongside deacons, priests, and laypeople from Episcopal churches, as well as seminarians and interns.

That kind of cooperative effort and presence tends to "foster contemplation," as he says. I assume the Rev. Prickett would agree that contemplating life and beliefs is always best as a two-way street. In other words, a person of faith might be challenged to reflect on the questions raised by a person who does not share their faith. This can save us from talking to ourselves.

I asked the Rev. Prickett if he views the secular worldview as a threat, a challenge, or an invitation to learn.

"Secular worldviews that promote one race, or one anything that inhibits treating our neighbors as ourselves, are a threat and a challenge because they do not present an invitation to learn. It must be noted that there are many religious views that are equally inhibiting."

A fascinating invitation to ask more questions—and build more bridges. Treating our neighbors as ourselves is a great step toward common ground. Of course, this teaching is not exclusively Christian, yet, whatever the origin, perhaps this is simply a quality of living a good human life, faith or no faith.

I appreciate that the Rev. Pickett recognizes that religious views can also inhibit our ethical ideals.

As a lover of nature, I enjoy asking religious believers what they think of the natural world and naturalistic views that do not accept supernatural beliefs. Prickett responded with classic Christian theology and a nice twist, "The world and all that are part of it are a creation of God. I love James Weldon Johnson's view: "And God stepped out on space and said 'I'm lonely', I'll make me a world." Prickett says you don't have to be a six-day creationist to feel "we are all responsible for maintaining [the earth] in perpetuity because God created it." This can be taken as another invitation to work together for our common home, whether or not we believe it came from a deity or a natural process.

Finally, I asked if he feels there is value in honest dialogue and cooperative action between people of faith and those without faith, and if this happens in his church.

"Without a doubt, conversations between all people are imperative if there is to be resolution of issues affecting everyone, and it does happen in our community."

The Rev. Prickett sent me a short piece on atheism written by Christian writer Frederick Buechner asserting that nonbelievers have no standards for ethics because, "With no God to point the way, humans must find their own way."

For me, this opens the door wide for much more dialogue and contemplation.

Thirty-eight
A Parable for Today

The purpose of a parable is to provide an image to carry along with us — a word-picture to make sense out of what seems so nonsensical at times. This essay is designed to invite people both with and without faith to default to "human-ness" by offering space to meet and discuss potential places to find agreement. (I'd like to see this scene in a film sometime.)

Some years ago when I was a parish associate in a beautiful church overlooking San Francisco Bay, I was teaching an Adult Study on "Scriptures of the World." It was fun to lead parishioners in readings and discussions of the Bhagavad Gita (Hindu), the Dhammapada (Buddhist), the Qur'an (Muslim), the Tao (Taoist) along with the only "holy book" they'd ever read — the Hebrew and Christian scriptures. I think it was during this class (I was also leading seven services each week in the county jail), I came up with a simple parable, which still seems relevant to our day.

The scene is a busy street corner in a teeming city (it could be your town or neighborhood). People are going about their business with movement, sound, and activity all around. A typical, ordinary day. Then ... an accident; a moment of crisis. An elderly lady falls in the street. Cars, trucks and buses screech to a halt. The stream of women, men, and children passing on the sidewalks stops. Everything stops, for a second. Then, everyone runs to help the fallen woman. All converge to assist. Strangers rush over from all directions (as we know, many usually just want to gawk, but many more want to help if they can).

Now, freeze the action.

Unknown to everyone there, the shopkeepers are a Baptist, a Buddhist, and a Hindu. The passersby are Muslim and Wiccan, Presbyterian and Unitarian. The drivers are Agnostic and Atheist, Catholic and Lutheran.

Police officers arrive. One is Episcopalian, the other, Jewish. An interfaith chaplain is riding along with the officers.

Emergency medical personnel race up—both women, both "Nones" (not affiliated with any religion). Among the responders are black and white citizens, Asian and Native American, Republican and Democrat.

The lady who fell—a recent immigrant from [anywhere].

A scene of crisis. What do people do? Do onlookers stop to think, "I don't know if that woman has the same beliefs that I do"? Do some say, "My political party is debating this kind of emergency assistance, I'd better wait for the decision"? Do others hesitate, thinking, "That woman isn't from here so I'm not going to help"? Does a young adult think, "Oh, that's just an old person; I don't care"?

Let's hope not.

I wonder how many religious folks would hold back for a minute to consider what their holy scriptures teach in these situations. Maybe someone would recall something about "helping the stranger." Do you think anyone would say, "Wait! I have to go check what my holy book says or what my pastor/priest/rabbi/imam tells me I should do!" Would someone kneel to pray asking, "What does God want me to do"?

Once, while I was riding my motorcycle through an intersection in front of my office, a lady ran a red light and smashed into me, sending me flying head over heels onto the pavement. My bike was totaled, but all I had was a few scrapes. Strangers appeared from sidewalks, cafés, and cars. Some came out on their porches and out of the library. Among the first to reach me was a pair of men who live on the street, whom I knew from chaplaincy work. They were concerned that I was okay.

Who is the stranger in these moments of crisis? Was I the stranger? Was anyone? Does anyone care what another person's religion, politics, race, or economic status is in these times? I highly doubt it. When we don't have time to let all our divisions and judgments influence our instinct to do the good and right thing, we do the good and right thing — at least I think we often do.

The best of our faith traditions teaches us to love our neighbor — care for the stranger. When another person is in need, sick, injured, vulnerable or weak, it seems most people are wired to show compassion — it's part of what makes us human. But how many consciously practice that thoughtful, caring compassion? In the secular community, there is talk of ethical responsibility, but how many live that in their lives? I think that among the faithful and the faithless there are many who do live their lives with concern for others. My sense is that we all want to help when we're needed; most of us will step in and step up to assist another person, even a stranger, when the situation calls for it. It's in our blood to act when we see another of flesh-and-blood suffering.

As strange as it seems, I wonder if we would do well to remember that we are all strangers. And that, in some sense, no one is. Those we may never know may need us, and we may, now or then, need them.

Thirty-nine
Is Your Family Divided by Faith?

There are few things more troubling about religion than the way it divides the human family. People make tribes, take sides, and then deride each other. It's bad enough when beliefs fracture a town, a state, a country, but probably the most disappointing is when a family is separated by the walls of faith. I've seen the destruction faith can cause up close for years: some of my family members went to their graves mad at a sister or brother or mother or father or cousin. Often it was some petty personal grudge or perceived slight, but lurking in the background was the shadow of divisive faith. I think in some ways this issue speaks to more readers in the Bible Belt, as close relationships and whole families can suffer from the belief that "God is on my side, not yours."

My older sister called recently. It had been a while. She wanted to tell me about a memorial service she went to for a relative. She lives out west and we don't see each other very often. Thousands of miles and "busy lives"—that eternal excuse—keep us apart, but there's another reason we don't talk that much: religion.

My sister called because she was thinking of the memorial, mortality, and me. She wanted to tell me she misses me and loves me. Life is short, so it's important to say what seems most important now, because later there may be no "later." I assured my dear sibling that I loved her too and said that even with our differences about some things, we'll always love each other as sister and brother. We ended the call a little choked up but cheerful.

How many families feel these relational rifts, these stresses and strains over sensitive beliefs? From what I can tell, a lot.

Those who wonder why an unbeliever thinks and writes so much about faith might want to keep this in mind: There may be no greater force of division in our world than dogma, doctrine, and divinity. Where are the reasonable voices echoing across the canyons that separate person from person, believer from unbeliever?

When a relative tells us they are praying for us, urges us to go to church (synagogue, mosque), or worries about our eternal soul, how do we respond? Anger and argument? Sadness, silence, or separation?

Let's do the math. Maybe you've read these figures before, but it's worth a reminder. The PEW Research Center, in its "Religious Landscape Study" from 2014, found that 70% of Americans identify as Christian. What's the next highest percentage? "Unaffiliated" (including atheists and agnostics) make up about 22% of Americans. That's way more than Jews, Muslims, Buddhists, Hindus, Mormons. No surprise, a higher percentage of the unaffiliated are young (18-29).

We may have heard all this before but it sinks in deeper when we think of relationships and families. One in five adults was raised in a mixed (or interfaith) family, so it's not uncommon for a family to consist of relatives who believe differently, either several religions or a person of faith and another with no faith.

This is our reality. Whether seculars like it or not, faith is "at home" in America. Whether believers like it or pray it's not true, nonbelievers are also "at home" here.

The real issue of concern is how these divisions play

out in our daily lives. Maybe it's not an issue for you and your family. But it probably is for your neighbor and many more in your town. It's certainly a national issue, as we can see every time a minority voice (including nonbelievers) speaks up for fairness. What we see—or maybe don't see enough—is the impact of the religious divide, the tensions that tear relationships apart.

We might ask ourselves if our beliefs are important enough to rip a friendship, a marriage, or a whole family asunder. As Jon Meacham writes in *American Gospel*:

"A Christian who opposes [an emotional cultural issue] sees any kind of accommodation as nothing less than a capitulation to the forces of death. A secularist who fears that believers blinded by faith will impose their values on the rest of the country thinks the religious rituals in public life may be the thin edge of the wedge."

We should all be aware of those wedges that divide us. Meacham observes that "Many committed secularists in our own age have largely made their peace with public religion." On the other hand, believers "ought to be more interested in making the life of the world gentle for others than in asserting the dominance of their own faith."

This might mean that an atheist lets some things slide (like "In God We Trust" and "God Bless America") while the person of faith tries to be a little more sensitive to the growing number of their "godless" neighbors. Obviously, religious congregations could learn from those who have left or choose to never go. Yet, that's risky and attitudes may change. Seems worth the risk though, doesn't it?

The risk is even more worth it when it comes to closer relationships, especially in families. If people can't find ways of communicating with open ears and open minds the fractures will fester. The sad conclusion will be: "My beliefs are more important than you."

In the hard work of listening with love, you can pick up a hammer, I can grab a saw, and we can make sure our fence has a gate.

Open fence, Purchase Knob, Smoky Mountains

Forty
Bridging the God-Gap

Continuing a favorite theme of bridges, I interview a Baptist pastor who also invited me out to a local café to deepen the conversation. With my own background, I wasn't surprised by anything he said, but there was a feeling of familiarity in our easy-going and honest back-and-forth. Some may wonder what the purpose of this is. What is accomplished? Is there a hidden agenda to change minds? I see the purpose as simply one of understanding and building relationships, which are, essentially, the most important bridges to construct, maintain and value.

Though I was raised in a Presbyterian church in north Seattle and was a leader of the youth group, I was invited by a girl I liked (you know teenage boys) to attend a youth gathering at her Baptist church. There was a small house next to the church where we all crowded in one evening to hear Fred, a dynamic young pastor, lead us in Bible study and prayer with a silly sense of humor. He made us all laugh or groan. New kids, like me, were introduced and welcomed.

At the end, when the doorway was crowded with kids, my friend and I slipped past and started down the walkway outside. "Chris!" — the pastor, surrounded by adoring youth, motioned for me to come back. I walked up the stairs where he shook my hand, pulled me close, looked into my eyes, and said, "I love you! See you next week."

Stunned, I left with my "church date." I continued coming to the fellowship, attending conferences and studies, until the church dismissed Fred. We all thought it was because he'd become too popular and maybe that threatened the church elders. We never found out. I never saw Fred again.

I tell this story because it's so vivid—an important moment of my youth, when a man, other than my dad, looked me in the eye and said he loved me. No pastor I'd ever known had said that to me.

Writing this column brought that memory back for me, as I recalled how powerful faith can be when it is expressed as love and acceptance.

I asked Johnny Prettyman, Lead Pastor of the Merrimon Avenue Baptist Church, now called Brookstone, how his faith tradition views nonbelievers. He replied, "In the traditional Christian faith, which I hold dear, agnostics, atheists, and secular people are described in the Bible as treasured lost sheep in need of the Good Shepherd."

His use of the word "traditional" caught my attention—something handed on from generation to generation. Beliefs, practices, and holy books are passed along so that those who follow will "hold dear" the essential teachings. Then the pastor gets "pastoral" with his response. He refers to the story of Jesus as the Good Shepherd who leaves the whole herd for one lost sheep. "Treasured lost sheep" reveals the sensitive care of both the pastor and the "Pastor."

I asked him if it is important to change the minds of nonbelievers. His answer was sharp: "I heard an atheist once say to Christians, 'How much do you have to hate a person to *not* try to change their minds about the most important issue in their life?' It is important to share our faith out of a heart of love, but the change of heart is the free choice of every individual."

The emphasis is once again on love as well as choice. As a secular person, I especially appreciate this emphasis. Free choice seems foundational to important decisions regarding matters of faith. If you really care about another person and you have a definite opinion about an important decision they face, you would try to help them to make the best choice for themselves.

The wider question would be, who really knows what is best for another person, and can we live with someone and love them if they freely choose an alternative view?

Pastor Prettyman told me that "a secular worldview is very normal and natural. I'm sure I was born with one. I do believe it was a threat to my soul and a challenge to change. I enjoy learning why people hold to secular worldviews." This was very honest and makes me want to know more, how "not believing" can feel threatening.

Regarding nature, the pastor explained, "God has given us [dominion, but], there is implied responsibility and stewardship. We need to take care of what He has given us. And as far as naturalism and the supernatural or science and faith … science has never disproved my faith."

As I see it, science cannot prove or disprove faith. Supernatural beliefs are beyond investigation. I would want to know more about that edge.

It was very encouraging to hear him say, "I think healthy dialogue is absolutely necessary between people of faith and without faith, and I don't believe it happens enough in our community. We are working on it, especially for the sake of needy people all around us."

When he encounters different perspectives, he is curious: "With all people I tend to question what it is they value in life and why."

I was grateful for this pastor's succinct responses and for his final word: "God Bless you as you seek to bridge a gap with the sacred and secular mindsets."

Forty-one
Francis of Assisi: Secular Saint?

Using the word "saint" is not something that comes naturally to me. Though I used to venerate the "heroes of faith," I found that the greatest models were countless common folks, not always the big names in belief. The concept of a saint came to mean a person who lived a compassionate life of pragmatism, loving and serving others with faith or without. They could cross any borders or boundaries that orthodoxy warns against.

My daughter was born in the City of Saint Francis (San Francisco) on, purportedly, his 800th birthday. Throughout my chaplaincy years in the Bay Area, I often reflected on the life and message of this remarkable person and always thought he was a good model for people of any faith, and for nonbelievers too.

Francis of Assisi (born around 1181) is known the world over as a Christian saint, a holy man, the Italian monk who founded the Franciscan Order. As the story goes, he gave up everything to rebuild a little ruined chapel brick by brick. He felt called to be poor and serve the poor. Not many seem "called" to do that kind of thing these days.

Francis is honored for his work with people in poverty but also for his famous Canticle of Creation giving thanks for Brother Sun, Sister Moon, and "Sister Earth, our Mother, who nourishes us and sustains us." Attending a Catholic Mass regularly while in seminary, I often sang his words, "Make Me an Instrument of Your Peace." The themes of care and service, concern for the earth, and living as a peacemaker still resound in our day.

There's a story of Francis I particularly like. He was wandering around one day feeling very happy. He asked an almond tree to tell him about God. Leaves shivered in the breeze and blossoms appeared. He passed by a creek and asked it to tell him of God: the waters bubbled and then became calm to reveal his reflected image. He met birds and asked them the same question: they sang to him. Then Francis met a pilgrim with a backpack and asked him, too. The pilgrim took him through the city to the area where poor people lived. The pilgrim sat on a bench, opened his pack and began to distribute bread to the people. He gave thanks, then he looked around and said, "Our bread." Francis understood. He had met something divine in the sharing of bread among the poorest.

This "preference for the poor" is one spark that has ignited liberation movements around the world. It's a practice of compassionate service going all the way back to the first lines of the Sermon on the Mount: "Blessed are the poor, for the kingdom of heaven belongs to them." I'm not sure why this clear statement is overlooked or ignored by many of his followers, but it may have to do with something I call "scripture scramble" — the word-play some use to scramble verses of the Bible to make it mean what they want it to mean.

As noted before, when Luke writes, "Blessed are the poor," and Matthew says, "Blessed are the poor *in spirit*," the scramblers say, "Aha! See, it's not about real poverty — this is a spiritual kind of thing." Some love to spiritualize everything. But what if the "kingdom" (the welcoming sanctuary) actually belongs to those who are really poor? Is that too uncomfortable to consider?

Along comes Francis, crazy enough to take Jesus's words seriously—to assume the most radical meaning. If centering relevant religion on poor folk is the main message, then this is not actually about theology at all. People can have their views of God and faith. But if the whole point is to respect and assist the poorest—if the heart of "good news" is the call for justice—then secular people are all in for this basic, grounded "new fundamentalism." It doesn't take faith to look people in the eye to share bread.

If other-worldly beliefs give way to this-worldly cooperation, Francis becomes not only a saint for one tradition but for all of us. Faith or no faith, we can build new "houses of god" from the ruins of the old because these will be real homes for those most in need of housing. "God's People" may simply be the most excluded outsiders and outcasts waiting to claim their rightful home.

Pope Francis—the first pope ever to take that name—spoke to a TED conference in April of 2017. He gently called for a revolution—a "revolution of tenderness." He said that he and his family were migrants in Argentina and he could have been "one of the discarded people." Through solidarity, humility and a sense of serving "the other," we can all practice the path of the saints: ordinary people doing extraordinary things.

A Franciscan priest in Brazil, Leonardo Boff, writes that Francis of Assisi shows us a "genius of seductive humanity and fascinating gentleness, which causes us to discover what is most true in our humanity. (*Saint*

Francis: A Model for Human Liberation; New York: Crossroads Publishing, 1982)

We can spend our time arguing religious doctrine or scrambled scriptures. Or we can learn from the gentle, tender revolution of either Francis, pope or saint, to listen to nature and share our bread.

Forty-two
Seeing What We Need to See

I often wonder who the people (or non-humans) might be who teach us to see, hear, and touch life more deeply. I want to pay attention to them and not miss their wise instruction — even if they never say a word.

Sometimes as I sit writing or thinking (or thinking about writing and writing about thinking) I catch a shadow out of the corner of my eye, a momentary movement nearby. I stop — at full attention. My senses tell me: Nature is close at hand; the Wild is visiting.

A favorite passage from Walt Whitman's *Leaves of Grass* says, "To glance with an eye or show a bean in its pod, confounds the learning of all times."

Hopping, slithering, flitting or lumbering by is a squirrel, rabbit, skink, or beetle, bumblebee, wasp, or butterfly of all descriptions. I observe and smile. A wren, cardinal, thrush, hummer, turkey. I watch, listen. Raccoon or bear. When the size startles me, I may forget to pick up my camera to click a pic. That can be a good thing — "catching a shot" can make me miss "catching the moment," what's happening right here, right now.

All this procession caught in a glance is distracting. In a good way. I lose my track, my train of thought, my flight of imagination. It keeps me from traveling somewhere else, as minds do so well.

Then, another sense kicks in and draws me back —

what distracts and attracts my attention is exactly what I need, just what I need to pay attention to. It makes me awake, alive, appreciative.

I may not be a naturalist but I do think of myself as a naturalistic thinker—naturally a nature person. I was distracted for a very long time by unnatural things, in fact, quite other-worldly things. What was "above the clouds" and "behind this world" and "beyond this life." Invisible things, imagined worlds, drew my glances away and I missed the goodness, beauty, and disturbing realities of this earthly life. My learning was "confounded."

While writing this a crawling motion by my foot grabbed my glance. A dark brown caterpillar with "eyes" on top of its head inched over and scootched under my shoe. I was glad I noticed. One movement of my foot and it would be squished.

My mind flashed to Sue, a woman I used to visit in her "home" under a freeway, a short walk from million-dollar houses. Sue knew me as a chaplain and I knew her as homeless, though she had her unusual, illegal campsite-home. One strong earthquake could crush her fragile dwelling along with Sue and all she owned.

Sue got cancer and died. The chaplaincy team and her community of the street held her memorial in the free dining room not far from her camp. One by one her friends told of Sue's generosity, caring and sense of humor shining through the darkness of her challenging life.

I'll always remember the first time I visited Sue at her home. Parking at the local Wendy's, glancing around to make sure no one saw me, I scurried up a muddy hill through thick bushes coming to a high fence: "State Property. No Trespassing." (My whole ministry sometimes seemed to be trespassing).

"Sue," I called out, not too loud. "Sue!" "Chaplain Chris?" came a voice from deep under the overpass. Sue emerged to show me the hidden passage through the fence. We walked up to enter her world, where she felt safe.

Walls of scrap wood, floor of old remnants of carpet. It was actually quite comfortable, though not quiet. I couldn't stand up completely, had to duck down a bit. I put my hand up to touch the "ceiling." Sue's roof was the freeway — I could feel the cold concrete vibrate each time a car raced passed a few feet above our heads.

I learned great lessons from Sue and her community. I became a part of that "congregation" of the concrete, that underworld of the alleys and bushes and hilly forests, of the cars and boats and shelters. A strangely great privilege. Each and all an urban refugee.

Reflecting on Sue, I wonder how many living beings are so close we can't see them — just out of sight, below, above, over there, out there. It's clear to me, often we don't really want to see. If we see we may feel the need to act, to do something, to take more care, to give something: our time, our attention. Some of what we choose to see might make so much of our lives seem irrelevant. We might be compelled to ask, "What am I missing in my distracted, confounded world?"

It's good to be distracted sometimes. Something by my foot called attention to something over my head (Sue's roof). We look down; we look up. What's going on here? Spiritual teachers have taught it but it's also a central secular lesson: What are we seeing? What are we not seeing?

Trailroots, Mountains-to-Sea Trail

Forty-three
The Freethinking Gospel of Frances Wright

It is a particular joy to recall some incident in my faith journey that seems to hold a lesson through the years – and to introduce another forgotten freethinker with wisdom for our day.

In teaching early American Freethought history from Paine through Burroughs and beyond, I have a lot of fun lifting up voices long forgotten in the dark corners. A powerful voice like Frances Wright's stirs some students to dive deeper into her revolutionary mind.

A number of years ago I was attending a multiracial congregation in the San Francisco bay area. Those folks stood with me when I was ordained. Rev. James Noel, the African American pastor, was a professor at my seminary and gave stirring sermons. White or black, the congregation frequently shouted an "Amen!" when he spoke "The Word" with a powerful emphasis on civil rights, justice, and compassion.

One Sunday, James was working into the crescendo of his homily when a scruffy-looking white man with a beard, sitting right in the middle of the sanctuary, began to speak loud and rough. The preacher paused and continued. The voice interrupted again. Some in the congregation turned to look, a little nervous at what would come next. Others sitting by the man, touched his arm and calmly whispered to him. Preacher James looked down from the pulpit at the man and said in a firm but gentle voice, "John, keep quiet now, this is My Time to speak." John sat back and settled down, squeezed between two elderly black women.

As it turned out, that church welcomed poor and homeless folks. They all knew John; he was an adopted member and they were used to his outbursts. It was one of the images, one of the stories, that nudged me toward chaplaincy in the jails and on the streets of that community.

When James left the church, I worked with a committee composed of black and white members as they called their first female pastor. Even with her Baptist background (this was a Protestant church), we decided she was the best candidate, and a great preacher just like James.

I mention this experience because it reminds us that, regardless of sex or race or denomination, some voices are warm and welcome; others are disturbing and disruptive. Some make us feel comfortable; others make us squirm. Some tell us what we expect to hear; some what we need to hear. When we are listening to these different voices it can sound like a cool, calming stream, or a chilling cascade. Maybe we need them both. What matters is that we listen.

Almost exactly 200 years ago, a woman appeared from Scotland with a voice that was both inviting and incisive. Her name was Frances Wright (1795-1852) and she brought a revitalizing message for the young nation that inspired many, while firing up fierce opposition. She conversed with Thomas Jefferson and befriended heroic Revolutionary War general, the Marquis de Lafayette.

One biographer tells us that "Wright's liberating influence had affected many aspects of American society from its religious to its educational institutions" (Susan Adams, foreword to *Reason, Religion and Morals*). Her achievements included working to end slavery; an experiment with interracial community near Memphis; advocacy of universal education and equal rights for women; supporting the rights of working people; and challenging capital punishment.

A major theme for this firebrand reformer was a call for citizens to return to the "shrine of human liberty" — the Declaration of Independence. What most energized Frances was that America wasn't living by its basic document, its fundamental principles. Denying rights to anyone because of race, gender, religion, no religion, or for any reason, was unreasonable and was denying the spirit of the "shrine."

Frances Wright had no tolerance for anything or anyone who stood in the way of reform and progress toward equality. To her, religious superstition and the power of religious authority were huge obstacles damming the stream of progress. She once said, "the true Bible is the book of Nature."

In her public speeches (some of the first speeches in this country by a woman before audiences of men) she was scathing in her exposure of religion's effect on the public mind:

"Let superstition spread her mists, and thick clouds of darkness; they shall be dispersed by the sun of knowledge."

"Orthodoxy owes all its strength to the disunion of the people [with its] silent and sectarian [congregating], in lieu of popular assembling in popular halls." (Wright converted an old church in New York to a "Hall of Science").

During her most eloquent speeches in Philadelphia and New York she unrolled a copy of the Declaration, held it up and proclaimed,

"Thus let us associate; not as Jews, not as Christians, not as Deists, not as believers, not as skeptics, not as poor, not as rich, not as artisans, not as merchants, not as lawyers, but as human beings, as fellow creatures, as American citizens, pledged to protect each other's rights—to advance each other's happiness." ("State of the Public Mind," 1829).

That's a voice strong enough to echo across two centuries. It's a voice and a "secular sermon" worthy to be preached. It may interrupt and disrupt, but doesn't Frances Wright's freethinking "gospel" have something to teach us today? Isn't it her time to speak?

Forty-four
When Suffering Comes to the Door

Finding common ground. It might sound simple, but we make it very complex at times. That we all experience suffering to some degree might just be a good way to step out on shared grounding.

Here are several stories that have shaped my life and my view of practicing a compassionate kind of humanity, even ministry, in environments of pain where faith is not necessary or essential.

Living in the mountains surrounding Asheville can feel like inhabiting a wildlife sanctuary. Every kind of furry and feathery neighbor comes to visit. As any humane human, I hate to see animals suffer. This morning I looked out on our patio to see one of our squirrel neighbors struggling to walk. I went to the window for a closer look and saw that it had either been attacked or was suffering from a disease. Chunks of fur were missing and it looked distressed. The squirrel limped toward the bushes, then stopped, turned, and crawled toward me near the window. I couldn't help thinking it was "asking" for help. It slowly disappeared into the vegetation. I felt helpless, though I know this is the cycle of life and death.

I've seen great suffering in my life. I've seen people waste away with cancer and other diseases, watched people kill themselves before my eyes—especially with drugs and alcohol—seen many suffer with mental illness and physical disability. My mother was wracked by pain from arthritis for as long as I can remember (she was the first person on the West Coast to have a double hip replacement operation—in the 1960s). Later, she had both knees replaced and then her wrists. I called her my "bionic mother." A strong woman.

As an instructor in a school for brain-injured adults, then as a chaplain in jails and streets, I got up-close and personal with mental illness, addiction, violence toward self and others—human pain in many forms and many faces.

How do we face pain and suffering, especially when it presents itself right in front of us where we can't turn away, we can't ignore or deny it?

Most of us, I think, respond with compassion. We may want to run away—"Let someone else handle this"—but we want to do something. We would end the pain and take away the suffering, if it was at all possible.

Some might, with good intentions, choose to pray. Nothing wrong with that. If a person wants to ask God for help—either to help the sufferer or to help the helper—who can criticize? Though some may use prayer as a retreat to protect themselves from facing pain or to "distract from the act" of helping, I think most people simply turn to someone else because they are at a loss at what to do.

Have you looked into the eyes of suffering? I know it sounds strange but the eyes of the dying squirrel brought this back to me today. We don't want to see it, but we have to sometimes.

As when Miguel stood behind steel bars in the county jail, inches from my face, to whisper his pain. Miguel's eyes filled with tears as he told me his son had just died—he couldn't be there to see his son for the last time.

Miguel asked if I would go to the house for him, to be with the family, to see his son. Without hesitation I said I would be honored.

Arriving at the house I saw people coming and going. As I walked in the open front door a relative greeted me, expecting me. Some friends were talking and eating in the dining room. Others were standing around laughing, telling stories. In the main room—the "living" room—was Miguel's son, laid out on the couch, clothed in jeans and a colorful shirt, surrounded by candles, incense, flowers. Soft rock music played.

As some watched, I sat by the body to gaze into the young man's face. Deep breaths reminded me to be present as Miguel's representative. As a father myself I felt tears well up as I placed my hand on the son's forehead. His skin felt clammy and cold but there was great beauty in that moment sensing this young life had known a loving family. Touching his body made me more human, more alive. Closing my eyes I knew this wasn't about me, not about faith or God, not really about suffering or death. It was real. It was good. Terribly sad, but good.

The next day when I entered the jail, Miguel was waiting at the bars. He grasped my hands, pausing in his gratefulness to feel the hands that had touched his dead son. It was a profound, life-giving moment for both of us.

A chaplain is privileged to stand or sit in these vulnerable moments. We suffer too. We can't always help—sometimes we shouldn't, if we think we can "rescue" or "fix" another's pain. But it helps to touch our own humanity, feel our own vulnerability, and look for hope in the eyes of another.

Unboxed turtle

Forty-five
Does Nature Care about Us?

Humans are funny creatures — funny, in strange ways. We rush around carrying our assumptions wherever we go. If and when we have a wake-up moment and stop to think, we might see that the universe does not revolve around us; we could learn some things by settling down to become a little more contemplative.

Here, naturalist John Muir makes an appearance to call our attention to the beauty all around us — something we should appreciate and respect since we're just a small part of it. And what if that beauty is what people have meant by the word "God"?

One morning I stepped outside and saw something in the road. As I walked down for a closer view, my fears were confirmed: a box turtle upside down in the roadway with a gash in the bottom of its shell. It was closed up tight, so I carried it to our yard, placing it right-side-up on a large rock. Thinking there was little chance it had survived, I went inside the house. After about 15 minutes I looked out and the rock was bare! I cautiously stole out to see the turtle standing in the flowerbed looking dazed but apparently okay. As I reached down, it hissed at me, pulling its head back inside. I left it alone. Next thing I knew it was crossing the driveway back toward the street, so I returned it to the bushes near where I found it.

Pleased that I am now known in the turtle-world as Savior of the Shell-People, I took a moment to reflect on why Nature can't protect all her creatures. Maybe she can't because there is no "she" to care.

When my "secular saint" John Muir (1838-1914) passed through WNC in 1867 on his famous thousand-mile walk (Indiana to Florida), he seemed most impressed with the "singing" he heard in the mountains:

"All the larger streams ... are mysteriously charming and beautiful ... and in the multitude of falls and rapids the wilderness finds a voice. Such a river is the Hiwassee, with its surface broken to a thousand sparkling gems, and its forest walls vine-draped and flowery as Eden. And how fine the song it sings!"

For Muir, all of nature was alive with creative energy, music, and a kind of dirty divinity. He saw "God" everywhere, but what or who was that? One of my favorite passages in his journals suggests, "The best synonym for God is Beauty." A perfect summary of his natural theology.

The Hiwassee runs from Georgia through North Carolina and into Tennessee. A great example of something we all know: rivers know no borders. Just like Muir's Beauty-God.

Of course, the world isn't always beautiful. There is suffering, disaster, death. But somehow we're always attracted, like John o' the mountains, to the awe-inspiring and beautiful, whether a high-country spring or a dragonfly wing.

Look at the odd ways we try to transform nature into a person and how that personality has many human characteristics.

The "fury" of a storm. The "raging" of the sea. The "fierceness" of lightning. An "angry" tornado. Or we speak of the "gentle caress" of a "whispering" wind or a "tranquil" stream.

"Acts of God" or "Mother Nature"? We think that somehow the weather, the sculpting movements of the earth, the creativity of great forces, show intention, will, emotion—a mindful hand controlling everything.

But what if nature doesn't care? What if there is no conscious personality pulling the strings, pushing the buttons—no wizard veiled by Oz?

Many seem to hold onto the ancient, primitive belief that the forces of nature are being moved by a divine hand that intends to please or to punish. But what if natural events are simply nature being nature, without a cause, purpose or meaning, without a thought for ridiculously small and (sorry) insignificant bipeds? What if the Mother Nature and Father God concepts are tricks we play on ourselves to feel better, to understand or explain who we are in the big scary universe?

When we're "blessed by a beautiful day" and the birds are singing "like a heavenly choir," while at the same moment of the same day somewhere else on the planet people are suffering and dying in floods or droughts, birds are silent as their forests are destroyed, and no one has the time to stop to see Beauty, God or much Good—what can we say?

I'm not sure it's best to say anything. But before we get too grateful for something great happening to us, thanking nature or praising God, we may just take a cue from Muir and write, reflect, quietly consider our lives, our world, without assuming we are special.

Our humility reminds us we are human ... made of humus. We can learn, with the earth as our classroom;

we can choose to care and practice daily empathy and compassion from a reasonable perspective. We can do what nature writ large cannot.

Maybe when it seems the Beauty-Nature-God is thinking of us, doing something for or against us, we need to listen to the songs Muir heard in the higher places. "The wilderness finds a voice." It may be only the winds, the waterfalls, and the wonders we behold — and, maybe that's enough.

Forty-six
Climbing Beyond Scripture

Being in the open air of the mountains can be a great opportunity to let go of the heavy things and thoughts that weigh us down and keep us back from moving forward and climbing up. I used to own shelf-loads of theological books including biblical study books. I gave them back to the seminary a long time ago, but I remember how they captivated my attention for years. Scriptures themselves can be heavy lifting for the mind, and I think it's worth the time for people of faith as well as the faithless to read the "wisdom literature" of the world's religions. Then, drop them, lighten the load, and forge ahead.

My brother flew in to visit from the "Left Coast," and naturally we decided to explore some trails in the Smokies and the Blue Ridge. We didn't see a soul for miles of meandering steps through forests where the only sounds were our breathing, an occasional bird, the wind in the tree-crowns, and bubbling rivulets. It's like hiking straight into Beauty itself. High on one ridge the thick woods suddenly opened to a wide view across rolling mountains, with streams flowing down and green flowing up into cottony clouds. We ate our simple snacks without many words. You just can't chatter much when a scene is so amazing. Two ravens swooped close, startling us with their swooshing wings before soaring onward and upward.

After walking miles in the wilds, my mind wanders to questions, both serious and playful. What are the names of all these mosses and trees ... and who cares what their names are? What would the First Peoples see and hear out in these wild places that I might be missing? Where are the owls hiding? What would we do if a bear suddenly stumbled out of hibernation and we were the first food it's seen in months?

I recall a pack-full of questions we pondered back in seminary days, when we were hiking around the Big Ideas that theology kicks up. The trail guide we used was called a bible, and one strange theme treks through the book like the long thread of the Appalachian Trail: "high places." What is it about high places that make some folks run to the summit while others run for cover?

Many of us can remember the major events in biblical history with these dramatic images: Moses on Mount Sinai, Elijah ascending Mount Carmel, Solomon building a high temple. The Prophet Isaiah sings, "How beautiful on the mountains are the feet of the one announcing peace" (52:7).

Then, much later, Jesus gives his famous "sermon" on the mountain, hears voices on the mount of "Transfiguration," climbs up the Mount of Olives and the cross of calvary. The expedition ends in The Revelation when the heavenly city appears in the sky and all believers hike up those golden trails into everlasting glory.

There's a lot of climbing going on it scripture. The whole story, beginning to end goes up and down—we almost need a mountaineer guide!

God is called "The Most High." God's home is above. No need to care about the lowly earth and the "fallen." What's *up* is what matters: think of the Greek gods of Olympus.

For many, it seems enlightenment comes on mountains (lightning and thin air may have something to do with that). For others, there is a dark side to mountains as well.

As ministry students we read about the dangers of "high places." The Lord seems very angry about what happens in some high areas. Take this verse from Leviticus when the Lord is demanding obedience. If the people don't obey, "I will destroy your high places" (26:30). Only officially-approved altars and sacrifices are acceptable.

Again, in the First Book of Kings, Solomon "sacrificed and offered incense at the high places" (3:3). That was okay, as long as the King was spilling the blood of thousands of animals to the Most High (the Highest God). Then, in the Second Book of Kings, Hezekiah "did what was right in the sight of the Lord" and "removed the high places, broke down the pillars, and cut down the sacred pole" (the pole Moses set up to heal the people—18:4). Who needs a high place when His Highness now camps in the lowlands?

Why do I drag out these ancient texts? Because very few people ever read these parts of the Bible, and even fewer realize how much mountains mattered centuries and millennia ago. In fact, we could say, faith came from mountain "highs."

Some people feel closer to God in the high country—high deserts, high plains, or high peaks. Others just feel closer to nature, and maybe themselves. A person may have faith to move mountains (First Corinthians 13) or even throw a mountain into the sea by praying (Mark 11:23), but we might wonder why a mountain can't simply be a mountain?

The alpine preacher of Palestine once said a thoughtful shepherd will leave a whole herd on the mountain to find the lost sheep (Matthew 18:12), but he climbed his last peak because, we're told, everyone is lost.

Here in the mountains of western North Carolina we have people who love the high places—even when we get lost sometimes—and there are those who say there is something higher.

I think I'll leave the heavy books behind and just keep climbing up.

The author seeking perspective, Blue Ridge Parkway   (photo by Carol Hovis)

Forty-seven
Theology for Beginners

*Naturalist John Burroughs once wrote that "theology shapes the universe with humanity as the center" (*The Light of Day*, 1900). That's a startling claim, since every theologian I've ever read puts God at the center. Burroughs was more honest, I think. Believers use lots of words and creeds and rituals to show God's greatness, yet somehow God's special concern in the universe is, you guessed it – humans. We are humbly the most important thing in the world and in God's eyes.*

"How is the person of tranquil wisdom [to live], who abides in divine contemplation? What are their words? What is their silence? What is their work?"

This line, from the ancient Hindu scripture, the Bhagavad Gita — "Song of the Lord" — is helpful when we consider our "words about God," or theology.

Anyone can seek wisdom, though few of us probably do. Contemplation is good, if we can calm down enough to do that. If we practice a peaceful wisdom and mindful reason, then what do we say, what do we do? Spiritual teachers across the centuries have told us where wisdom can be found (mostly in wise teachers like them), how to contemplate, meditate, and cogitate. Some tell us what to say and what to do. Yet, as the Gita suggests, the missing piece may be: "What is their silence?"

Could it be that our greatest teachers are the ones who know how to be silent? In my evangelical college days a professor passed along this quote I've never forgotten: "The greatest teacher is the one who teaches others to be self-taught." When I read Emerson's *Self-Reliance* I heard the same wisdom (he read the Gita too). We might keep in mind that a lot of famous teachers of religion who base their words on famous old books may not know more than anyone else in these matters. Hold that thought.

Here's a simplistic summary of the world's major religious philosophies, and I hope you'll see I'm bringing a little humor into it (with apologies to the scholars).

Taoist (ancient Chinese): Follow the Path. The Path cannot be told. Honor the Dead. There is no death. Balance your imbalance. Earth and Heaven are One.

Jewish: The Best God of all gods, Who has no Name, moves around (gardens, mountains, deserts, temples). God chose one group of people to move with Him. They all moved to one place to settle. It was a very unsettled place.

Christian: God sent God so that God would die to please God. God is Love. God made hell for those who don't love Him.

Muslim: God is greater than all religions and prophets. Our religion and prophet are the greatest.

Hindu: Many Gods. Many Paths to Many Gods. Many Gurus (teachers). Be your own Guru. God is Nothing — God is Everything.

Buddhist: Wake up! Maybe you are God but if there is no God you are not God. There is no Buddha but there is "buddha" (awakening) and you are a buddha. Learn to laugh. Buddha laughs too (if there is a Buddha).

I told you this was simple, and I hope it causes smiles. But the serious side is this. Definitions of "God" are all over the map of history. Who decides what "God" is and who decides who decides these things? Does Religion create Theology or does Theology beget Religion? What comes first, the chicken or the universe?

Some describe God as "ineffable" (indescribable). Others use lots of words to say that God is "transcendent" (above and beyond words). Yet others tell us that God is "infinite," "unknowable" or "unsearchable" (theology uses a lot of negatives). But then they fill whole libraries with books about who God is, what God thinks and feels, who God likes and doesn't like. Confusing, isn't it?

Theologians are professional guessers. I've known some. I hear their objections. "Now wait a minute! I've studied the ancient words and I've read all the other theologians. So I'm NOT guessing!" I would smile and calmly reply, "So, you're telling us you know something about Someone we can't see, based on what people have said over thousands of years?"

Hindu theology offers a way out of getting too serious about our theologies. It teaches that the divine is "Not this; not this." Is this God or is this God? Not this; not that. How does a theologian handle that?

Psalm 146:7 presents a practical theology-beyond-theology: The Lord "executes justice for the oppressed; gives food to the hungry; sets the prisoners free ... watches over strangers; upholds the orphan and widow."

Or take the verses that I first heard as a "call to ministry": "Is not this the fast [religious duty] that I choose: to loose the bonds of injustice ... share your bread with the hungry; bring the homeless poor into your house." [Isaiah 58] Is this true theology?

John Burroughs wrote, "People are ... coming to see that devotion to the truth is the essence of true religion, and that the worst form of irreligion is the acceptance of creeds and forms without examining them, or upon the sole authority of some book or sect [or authority]" (*Accepting the Universe*).

Looks like we're all beginners with these things.

Forty-eight
Kitty Hawk, Curiosity, and an Ethic of Care

If we're reflective people, our experiences in life can be teaching moments. In our travels across oceans or mountains or even across our towns, we may find how similar we are to others. One local pastor to whom I gave the "secular quiz" offered some hints at what could happen when believers and nonbelievers communicate, cooperate, and practice an ethical way of life.

Carol and I enjoyed a stunning drive to the Outer Banks, up through Virginia and down the always spectacular Blue Ridge. We love the endless beauty of nature, and we're also drawn to historic sites to learn more of who we are as a nation.

I'd always wanted to visit Kitty Hawk and see the place where the Wright Brothers first turned humans into birds. My father built 747s near Seattle for many years, so this trip felt like a pilgrimage honoring his memory. To walk the 120 feet of the historic first flight that took place one December morning in 1903 was emotional. The 12-second soar from Kill Devil Hill opened the skies to the reach of invention and imagination.

At Kitty Hawk I picked up a copy of David McCullough's book, *The Wright Brothers*. Reading the early life of Wilbur and Orville, I was delighted to find that their mother supported the boys' inventiveness and their father, a United Brethren bishop, encouraged wide reading of books, even the works of Robert Green Ingersoll.

As McCullough puts it, "It was the influence of Ingersoll apparently that led the brothers to give up regular attendance at church, a change the Bishop seems to have accepted without protest."

Many years later a friend said the brothers were examples of how people without special advantages can do great things. Orville said that wasn't true. They did have an advantage. "The greatest thing in our favor was growing up in a family where there was always much encouragement to intellectual curiosity."

This kind of curiosity leads me to continue my "series" asking local clergy how they view secular, nonbelieving people ... those who may not fly with the flock.

Back in Asheville, I asked the Rev. Marcia Mount Shoop, pastor at Grace Covenant Presbyterian Church, how her faith tradition views nonbelievers. She said there is no "monolithic view of nonbelievers" because there are "viewpoints all along the theological continuum between the extremes." She explained that "Christ is unique" but there is a "mysterious and expansive grace of God." She went on, "The nature of actual relationships with nonbelievers probably tends to lean in a 'let's-not-talk-about-the-hard-questions' direction with people who don't believe."

Mount Shoop says her congregation "embraces mutual learning," and that personally she has "learned a lot about my faith from my relationships with people in other faiths and with people who do not understand themselves as believers." This seems quite hopeful as a step across the sands and shores of belief.

I asked if she sees secular worldviews as a threat. "I believe religious extremism is a threat. Secular worldviews I do not encounter as a threat." This seems reasonable. Then she spoke of science as one secular worldview, and my ears perked up. She feels that science has a lot to teach; "however, there is a danger that science is seen as an infallible source of answers when it positions itself as a secular alternative for certainty" that some religious people claim. "I don't think science has all the answers."

Here is where I would offer a balance. The scientific method is not about certainty or being infallible but, rather, seeking to find evidence of what is true about the universe. In fact, science is not really a "secular worldview" (there are many believing scientists) or a worldview at all. Scientists don't claim they have final answers to questions outside their particular field of investigation (biologists don't claim they know astronomy). "Thankfully," Rev. Marcia says, "science does not threaten my faith." She affirms, "Science and my faith together help me discern healthy, life-giving ways of being in the world."

She went on: "The belief that science is all we need or can answer all of life's questions ... does at times diminish our public discourse...." I would agree, if this were the case. But once again, I don't hear these claims about science—from scientists. However, science and philosophy (reason) are fairly fundamental tools to understand our world. "Life's questions" are open-ended. Faith is one response, yet certainly doesn't provide "all the answers" or "certainty" either.

It was good to hear her acknowledge that "Nature

is our teacher" and "our home," and since "creation is sacred," her faith informs an "ethic of care [and] interdependence."

The last question I posed concerned dialogue and cooperation. She said, "Cooperative action is at work in Asheville," yet, "There are divides ... that need healing." I appreciated the invitation implied by her final comment: "The relationships between people of faith and [nonbelievers] may well be one [divide] that I have not seen yet."

Perhaps the inventive imagination of Kitty Hawk will encourage further soaring across any divides.

Forty-nine
Proverbs from the Sea-Island Gullah

Indigenous people are the real locals and, often, the best storytellers. If we make the time to listen and take the opportunity to learn some "alternative history," there are treasures to be had.

Living in the South with a sensitive ear to the history of slavery is a two-edged sword. We look for ways to soak in the historical events on Civil War battlefields, in books and films, but we are appalled and horrified by much of the story. We seek to learn more, but it's painful. White folk, like me, can only imagine what African Americans have endured for 400 years, but we don't have to imagine – we can meet people, hear, and learn.

"Every frog praise e ownt pond" (Every frog praises its own pond).

This proverb from the Sea Island People – the Gullah or Geechee, descendants of African slaves – draws attention to the places and faces we most value.

When we were visiting Gullah communities off the coast of South Carolina we were privileged to hear a good-natured Geechee man describe his culture, history, and language. He drove us through the "ponds" of modest homes in these island communities squeezed and surrounded by larger homes of mainlanders. Resort development is rapidly eating up the valuable coastal land.

As we listened and learned, our guide, David

Campbell, explained the difference between the "Binya" and the "Comya." A Binya is an island native (one who has "been here") and a Comya is one who has "come here" from another place, the mainland.

David was light and humorous about it, but the historical tension is wrenching. As in so many indigenous cultures, the Comya changed the land and the culture of these proud people, who now number about a half million. Thankfully, the Gullah, like David and his family, are not going to let their story be forgotten or ignored, no matter how much the pond is drained or muddied.

"E mout na know no Sunday" (His/Her mouth doesn't know Sunday—a day of rest). We hear lots of talk about cultural diversity and racial equality and it's essential that we hear it. But sometimes it may be good to give our mouths a rest and listen—listen to the stories even if (and especially when) those stories show us a shadow side to our own story.

Gullah people have a deep spiritual tradition rooted in Africa. They pay attention to dreams and meditations and their "root doctors" use plants and roots as medicine. The comya church came in after slavery to convert the islanders, dressing up the Geechee as good Christian Americans.

In his 2008 book, *Gullah Cultural Legacies*, David's brother Emory Campbell explains:

> Just as we made efforts at home to change our hair and skin texture to become more 'acceptable' to other Americans, [our school] was exhorting its students to 'get cultured.' The school was teaching them to look and act like European-Americans

so that they would be accepted as mainstream Americans. (Hilton Head, SC: Gullah Heritage Consulting Services, 2008).

I heard an echo of this from Timothy, an Ethiopian friend who exchanges emails with me. He's a young college graduate finding it very hard to live or find work in his homeland. The other day Timothy wrote to tell me he spends his days with artists while "going through contemplation with the Rural." He recommends the famous Ethiopian singer, "Teddy Afro," who "preaches our tears of justice and frustration." Timothy closed his email with, "I keep my ears with him."

"I keep my ears with him." When your mouth knows Sunday and you can stop hopping around in praise of your own pond, maybe you hear what you need to hear. Like wisdom from Africa.

Closer to home, my wife was deeply impressed by our local "Hood Huggers" tour with its rolling classroom driving through African American neighborhoods rich in stories.

"New broom sweeps clean but old broom gets the corners" (a new person may seem to have all the answers, but the Binya knows better what needs to be done). How many times have we heard of missionaries who try to come in and sweep an entire culture away to impose their own ways on people? They may use nice words and may even have good intentions, yet their brooms (beliefs, Bibles, clothing, religious education) can be weapons. If we "keep our ears" with the original inhabitants we still hear their voices of survival, resilience, and cultural pride.

Emory Campbell explains: "Being constantly mistaken as one from the continent of Africa confirms the fact that there is a true connection between Gullah people and Africans who had never left the continent. We are descendants of enslaved people brought from Africa some 400 years ago, who have retained Africanisms in our speech, food ways, and daily ways of living." And celebrated in delightful proverbs.

It's amazing to me that we can, even now, visit the Eastern islands and hear a Gullah woman, man, or child greet us with a smile and a "How oonah da do?" (How you all doing?). If we're honest about our history we will learn from other histories. I want to ask, "How are you doing, after what you've endured, after they came to make you look and sound and believe like them? Tell us your story." Because their story of tragedy and triumph is somehow my story, our story.

"E head da run ainty?" (Is he/she thinking clearly?). Are we?

Fifty
Walt Whitman, Chaplain

"There will soon be no more priests ... a new order shall arise ... and every person shall be their own priest" (Preface, Leaves of Grass*, 1855 edition).*

He's been called America's poet and no poet at all. Some have even called him a Christ-figure while others have called him everything but the antichrist (and maybe that too). Angel or devil or maybe a mix of both. He'd love it all.

Walt Whitman. Born on Long Island, journalist in Brooklyn, clerk in Washington, D.C. during the Civil War, he was attracted to the wildness in city and countryside.

A child brought him a handful of grass and his life-work was born. A revolution in literature, *Leaves of Grass* first appeared in 1855. Hardly anyone cared or dared to read it, except one of the great minds of the time, Ralph Waldo Emerson, who wrote to the young poet, "I find it the most extraordinary piece of wit and wisdom that America has yet contributed ... I greet you at the beginning of a great career." The literary genius met the poetic genius and the spark was kindled.

Fired from his job as clerk at the Interior Department (the Secretary was horrified the author of "that book" worked for him), Walt went on to work in the Attorney General's office. Yet his heart was with the wounded soldiers in the national capitol, a city that had become "one vast central hospital."

In my years as a chaplain I often went back to thumb through Walt's mind and words (he said his book was identical to himself). I always have been impressed by his service among the wounded and dying. He seems to me the perfect example of good chaplaincy or any relevant ministry. He willingly walked into suffering and became a model for anyone seeking to be a companion for others in their suffering.

"During those three years in hospital, camp or field, I made over six hundred visits or tours, and went, as I estimate, counting all, among from eighty thousand to a hundred thousand of the wounded and sick." He comforted everyone, Northerner or Southerner.

"In my visits to the hospitals I found it was in the simple matter of personal presence, and emanating ordinary cheer and magnetism, that I succeeded and helped more than ... anything else." (*Memoranda*) His small pack and bulging pockets were often full of gifts for the men including fruit, pencils, magazines and books. The greatest gift he brought was himself.

Walt first served with the Christian Commission but when it became obvious they were more interested in saving the souls of soldiers than bringing "real aid," he went on his own. His brother, George Washington Whitman, had been wounded at Fredericksburg so Walt knew the infirm needed a different quality of "soul care."

Whitman was no atheist. But how do we make sense of his beliefs?

"My faith is the greatest of faiths and the least of faiths, enclosing all worship ancient and modern," he writes in *Song of Myself*, 43. Later (48) he speaks bluntly: "And nothing, not God, is greater to one than one's self is."

Those most shocked by these statements need to press on to hear the full message of the prophetic poet:

"I call to mankind, Be not curious about God … I am not curious about God … I hear and behold God in every object, yet I understand God not in the least."

Honesty is one major quality of effective chaplaincy.

"In the faces of men and women I see God, and in my own face in the glass; I find letters from God dropped in the street, and every one is signed by God's name."

For Walt, any "God" must include everything and everyone.

Where do we root him in religion? A deeper question may be: What is below, under the beliefs, beneath the traditions people hold so tightly to? Walt digs down to deeper roots. He finds anything divine in the earth, and in "comrades" who, like him, are "absorbed" (a favorite word for the poet) into a messy but common humanity—sensual and suffering—intertwined in the beauty of the "Kosmos."

"Every atom belonging to me as good belongs to you" (*Song of Myself, 1*).

Walt didn't throw out divinity, faith or scriptures. He simply absorbed it all. He found all that within himself and became his own priest, his own chaplain.

Many people have tried to ignore or even censor Walt Whitman. I find that strange for one main reason: He was a practicing chaplain who loved his own life and Life itself. I would think we would want to have more of that living poetry in our contemporary lives.

Stormclouds over the Blue Ridge

Fifty-one
Facing Disasters, with Faith or without

This column was written during a period when every day brought news of some new disaster, some local, some far across the globe. What better time could there be to consider humanity in such thrall to nature? This may fly in the face of thousands of years of history, mystery and myth, but a fresh consideration of the Four Elements can remind us of our human fragility and bring us back down to the basics of earthly life, and death.

More than fifty years later, I remember scrambling under the desk in my suburban Seattle school the morning of the 1964 Alaskan earthquake—the one that moved the continent a fraction of an inch. Almost as scary as our nuclear attack drills.

A quarter of a century after that, my daughter and I were shaken—literally and figuratively—by the 1989 earthquake in San Francisco when over fifty people died and part of the Bay Bridge collapsed. We huddled in a doorway of our cheaply made apartment (built on landfill) and cried as the walls swayed and bookshelves fell. It was a scary fifteen seconds.

Carol and I followed the fires in the Bay Area intently as some of our friends and colleagues evacuated their homes and watched neighborhoods burn to ashes. It was very emotional even from a distance.

Most of us have felt the fear of these tense moments.

How many of us have faced natural disasters in one form or another? (Human-caused tragedy is another story.) When this essay was written late in 2017, we had watched an endless series of terrible natural events, from hurricanes to earthquakes, floods and fires. A continual barrage of images and stories from Houston to Mexico, from Puerto Rico to Northern California, and faraway centers of suffering. Sometimes it seems we're members of the Disaster-a-Day club. Will it ever stop? We know it won't, as long as we're holding on for dear life to this rock spinning wildly through space.

I've been reflecting on the Four Elements and how they can seem at times to be out to get us. Air/Wind—hurricanes and tornadoes; Water—floods and tsunamis; Earth—quakes and landslides; Fire—volcanoes and firestorms.

The ancient Greeks gave each element a name and a god. The Wind was the winged Eurus with Zephyr and friends controlling the Four Winds. Poseidon (Neptune to the Romans) handled all things Water, ruling the ocean. Earth was Gaia, the Mother of all material things. Fire was the realm and responsibility of Hephaestus (Vulcan to the Romans).

The word "dis-aster" originates in the Latin: "bad star," maybe related to our expressions "not in the stars," or even "under a dark cloud." "Somebody up there doesn't like us" might be a similar phrase.

We try to make sense out of destruction, especially faced with the awesome power of nature. For thousands of years we've attempted to put a human face on the elements so we can better comprehend the incomprehensible. It can't simply be a natural thing, it has to be the work of a heavenly hand.

One rather odd thing about disastrous events is they, more than just about anything else, reveal our latent superstitious nature. We can almost predict responses that turn a natural event into a "lesson," a "test" or a "message" from the divine. Some go so far as to credit God when one person survives a calamity while others die. We sometimes hear the claim that a weather or geologic event is some kind of judgment or punishment, usually directed toward unbelievers or other "unrighteous" people.

Ancient people were very superstitious, believing that "the gods" were angry or pleased, bringing peace or war, prosperity or ruin. It appears to me that at least part of the history of religion can be explained by appeasing and pleasing the powers so they won't be upset enough to throw lightning bolts.

Where does the responsibility lie with disasters? It depends on lots of things, but as I see it, blaming them on the forces of Good or Evil doesn't really help. It deflects the responsibility and disrespects nature itself. Shoddy housing construction may lead to many deaths in an earthquake. Poor planning or building in a flood plain may have terrible consequences. But we can't blame some other Someone somewhere. We may not understand, but that doesn't mean we can get away with claiming or blaming a god.

Awful and awesome things that happen to us and our world might serve to remind us that we're not in control—and that nature is greater (almost a "statement of faith" for me, one that requires no belief). We are made of the Four Elements, so any one of them can help or harm us at any time. If we're honest with ourselves, we are only an infinitesimal part of nature.

For those who believe in God, disasters present a difficult dilemma chock-full of questions: Why do terrible things happen? Why doesn't God stop them? Why aren't prayers answered for so many?

For them, and for those who do not believe, we can ask: What can we learn from the kindness and selflessness we see when disaster strikes?

Perhaps people with faith or without faith can find something to agree upon here. If we leave out the superstitions we can face adversity and the questions together.

Fifty-two
So You Believe or Don't Believe — Then What?

A reader of my column asked a not uncommon question: How can a person who doesn't believe in God be ethical or even have a conscience? This led to a short exchange on my blog. As is often the case in online "discussions," the reader merely quoted two "authorities" — the Bible and Billy Graham — and disappeared. My obvious response was that I didn't accept those as authoritative, but I did appreciate the comment that faith was no guarantee a person would be good or ethical.

Where does faith lead? Where does unbelief lead? Exploring the ultimate intent makes a lot of sense.

Neil Carter is a former evangelical Christian who writes a blog on the religion site, Patheos, called "Godless in Dixie." Neil is a schoolteacher and father of five who moderates a discussion group of more than 450 atheists in Mississippi.

A few years ago Neil was interviewed by a pastor for "Interview an Atheist at Church Day"; the video of the interview has had more than 200,000 views. That video got me asking a question I often ask myself: What if? What if more congregations dared to move beyond the fear and misunderstandings to invite secular people in for conversation, questions, and dialogue? Some may ask, "What's the purpose? To doubt our faith?"

I suppose the answer depends on the congregation

and how people understand the value of asking hard questions of ourselves.

For many people the word "atheist" conjures up a whole lot of negative images and feelings. "Atheists hate religion and faith"; "Atheists are angry with God"; "Atheists are unhappy people"; "Atheists are un-American." You may have heard something like this, or felt that yourself.

Nonbelievers like Neil Carter (and many of the 800 members of The Clergy Project) offer an alternate view, a different perspective, on the choice to disbelieve.

In one blog post Neil writes, "*Atheism for Dummies* author Dale McGowan once said that 'Atheism is the first step. Humanism is the thousand steps that follow.' I totally agree.... Atheism is just the beginning. It's only an answer to one single question: Do you believe in any gods? Speaking for myself, I'm far more interested in where you take things from there."

In other words, a believer says "I believe" and a nonbeliever says, "I don't believe." Then what? Does that shut down all conversation? Does that create an insurmountable obstacle to any relationship or potential to work together? Why can't that be the opening for some very healthy exchanges in order to do what good dialogue is meant to do: to learn, to gain understanding, to consider how another person thinks or feels?

Not long ago a student asked me to "tell us more about your personal story." I smiled and replied that the class was not about me but Freethinkers in history, but, I assured him, "You'll hear a lot of me in telling their stories."

That's the point, isn't it? We learn from history as

well as the histories all around us. We all have stories to tell and often we find there are commonalities, parallels in some elements of our personal journeys. Statements of belief or faith only tell so much of the story. Who the person is behind the belief or nonbelief is interesting as well, or it ought to be. A story of conversion as well as de-conversion is deeply personal and meaningful to each of us. Where can we share those stories safely without judgement?

Theist or atheist, that is the question. But it's only one question—only a beginning. Like Neil, I'm "far more interested in where you take things from there." I'm as unimpressed by someone who makes it all about their faithlessness as I am by someone who makes it all about their faith. We need more teaching and less preaching.

You may have noticed that most discussions of atheism focus on what's missing, what someone does not have. No god. No faith. No community or congregation. Many assume this means a nonbeliever also has no hope, no peace, no love in their lives. At its worst, this can lead to the prejudice that nonbelievers have no morality since "they have no moral standard." Atheists often respond with a question: "You mean if you didn't have the Bible telling you how to be good you wouldn't know that killing, stealing, or treating others unjustly is wrong?" Ethical practice is essential to Humanism and that's why the phrase "Good without God" is popular. This isn't to say people who believe in God are not good. It only needs to be said to counter the misnomer that you need God in order to live a life of goodness and love.

There is so much more to the story that needs to be heard. As Neil explains in his video at the church, the more we talk about these things in the open, we find we share many of the same values and "beliefs" about what is good and right and important for our communities. And thus the more we understand each other.

Freethinkers (atheist and agnostic) live and work alongside faithful believers in the same communities. What if we put aside some fears and listened more?

It may be time for more "Interviews with an Atheist at Church." Then again, I might suggest creative alternatives such as "Sacred Secular Sunday" or "Freethought Friday Forum." Whatever it's called, I have no doubt it will be a valuable experience of education and bridge-building.

Path to the Unknown, Blue Ridge Mountains

Afterword
Seeking Truth with Lucretia Mott

Truth for Authority, not Authority for Truth.
— Lucretia Mott

One of my "freethinking saints" is Lucretia Mott (1793-1880), a Quaker preacher of abolition, women's rights and freethought. She was proud of being called a heretic and infidel. Cousin of Benjamin Franklin, friend of Elizabeth Cady Stanton, colleague of Frederick Douglass, she was a force to reckon with as she worked tirelessly for equality, justice, and freedom.

Truth was central for Lucretia Mott. As a founding member of several Society of Friends meetings and women's rights conventions, she believed that truth was more than a principle or philosophy: it was the basis for a way of life, fierce yet non-violent, regardless of one's religious beliefs. Truth could be found as an "inner light" within the individual's conscience: the mind or "soul," guided by experience and common sense, was the ground of authority. No orthodox individual or institution controlled the authoritative truth.

When some Quakers used scripture in support of their views, she countered with her personal motto: "Truth for Authority, not Authority for Truth." It is no surprise she was reviled as "a most dangerous woman." Though a person of deep personal faith, she needed no book or tradition to find her way and speak her mind, and she became a model for all reformers—freethinkers with faith or without.

In the history of religion we hear lots of amazing stories. We hear tales of ordinary men (primarily men) who walk out of deserts and forests, caves and fields, with news to proclaim, curious experiences and messages to announce. They try to convince anyone who will listen that their extraordinary experience really happened. If we were there among the first people to hear these incredible stories, would *we* find them credible? How would we know we weren't hearing fake news, even if the reporter seemed convincing, sincere, believable?

In today's world, bombarded by claims of "fake news," could Lucretia help us discern whom or what to trust? Objective things are happening, they're just seen or reported from a spectrum of subjective viewpoints. If news, like truth and beauty, is in the eye of the beholder—real or fake according to each person's particular perspective—how we can absorb and make sense of the waves of information and "reports" rolling in from across the globe, other than by relying on wisdom like hers?

Let's consider what news we hear from the world of faith and religion.

We have to begin, of course, with the ancient sources of news (though not so new for us)—tales, texts, and "truths" from our diverse faith traditions. There is "new" news from religious reporting services, denominational bulletins, and online sources such as Beliefnet and Patheos. "Guiding light" comes from faith-based magazines, books, blogs, podcasts and television shows—as well as from religion pages in newspapers and "authoritative" messages from pulpits everywhere.

Some of these sources tell us they have "breaking news" — not only "good news," but the "best news." It's always breaking and dramatic — more like a reality show than a sincere exploration of beliefs. It's as if they are saying there is only one channel, one show, that's really worth watching. I'd call that broken news, and maybe not news at all.

I listened to a "Radiolab" podcast that was a little scary. New software can manipulate the words and facial movements of a person on-screen, literally putting any words you choose into their mouth. You could have a performer, politician, or preacher saying whatever you want them to say, and it would be almost impossible for most of us to notice.

Talk about "breaking" and broken news. Doesn't this make it even more urgent for us to know truth when we see it, or hear it? We need the will to suspend judgment and suspend belief; to take time to contemplate and investigate; to listen to our own "inner light," as Lucretia called it.

This is a challenge for both believers and nonbelievers who think there really is "truth" (and not always in quotation marks) to be found in our common world. We ask ourselves: Do we trust a source? If experience tells us the person is trustworthy, that their report is most probably accurate, then it should be fine to accept what they say as true. But knowing this — really knowing — still seems slippery.

No one's an expert on this search for accurate information (remembering that information is not knowledge and knowledge is not wisdom). We might say, "I heard it on __" or "I saw it on __" or "I read it in the __." Or we claim, "__ said it, it must be true." We all do it: liberals, conservatives, the faithful and the faithless: we love to hear "news" and then pass it along, because we love to make the news our own, to present ourselves as a knowledgeable source.

But we can't leave truth a blank. Like it or not, we need each other to serve as testers of truths told. I make it a practice to say, "I heard this ... but I'm not so sure."

The immensity of nature can be immensely helpful and instructive—even authoritative—in these matters.

When I walk along a deep forest path, my senses are heightened—at full alert, wide open. So is the wildness of imagination. That shadow looks like an owl; that rock looks like a bear. Is that a bird or a human voice? Is that a root ... or a snake in the trail?

This may give us a hint along our stumbling, humbling trail toward truth. If we are to use our senses—and our common sense—to determine what's really going on beyond the mistakes and fakes, we may want to keep these rules of thumb in our packs and pockets:

- ask lots of questions;
- don't jump to judgment (one way or another);
- take a deep breath, step back and wonder;
- check it out;
- think and reason;
- ask more questions;
- give freethinking a try.

I suspect we'll be okay, if we can remember these simple tools to test the true.

Then again, the tools aren't too simple. We might not want to carry such a heavy pack. One thing is true: the truth has never been too easy. Naturally difficult, but not impossible. It may be much harder to figure out tomorrow than it is today. It seems worth the effort, though.

Lucretia Mott liked to quote the line attributed to Jesus: "You shall know the truth and the truth shall make you free." Yet, how do we really "know"? That is the central question, one we must ask over and over.

Setting aside that some traditions would have us believe a person, a book, or a creed embodies freedom and truth, we can happily take the ancient teaching as a call for all freethinkers—in the sacred or secular worlds—to figure out what is true and how to live it freely. As I see it, there really is only one world, and truthfully, it's pretty good.

Lucretia, and perhaps Jesus, might cast a knowing smile with these truthful words from a poet, chaplain and happy heretic:

You shall not look through my eyes either, nor take things from me; You shall listen to all sides and filter them from yourself.
—Walt Whitman

The author (photo by Carol Hovis)

About the Author

Chris Highland grew up in the Pacific Northwest and lived for over 35 years in the San Francisco Bay Area. He was a Protestant minister and Interfaith chaplain for many years before becoming a Humanist celebrant.

With a degree in Religion and Philosophy from an evangelical Christian university (Seattle Pacific) and a Master of Divinity degree from a diverse consortium of seminaries (Graduate Theological Union in Berkeley), he has been active in "presence ministry" and nonprofit work in a private school, a county jail, homeless shelters, and affordable housing.

He is the author of ten books including *Meditations of John Muir, My Address is a River, Life After Faith*, the novella *Jesus and John Muir*, as well as an e-book essay collection, *Nature is Enough*. He has taught courses on Nature Literature and Freethought in California and North Carolina.

Chris blogs at Secular Chaplain and, as a member of The Clergy Project, he contributes to Rational Doubt on Patheos. Seeking wider connections, he also holds membership in the American Humanist Association, Americans United for Separation of Church and State, the Religious Naturalist Association, and the Freedom from Religion Foundation.

Since 2016 he has been writing weekly "Highland Views" columns for the Asheville *Citizen-Times* (a *USA Today* affiliate) addressing major religious and theological questions as well as sensitive issues of faith.

Chris and his wife Carol, a Presbyterian minister, live in Asheville, North Carolina. His website is www.chighland.com.

Also available from Pisgah Press

Mombie: The Zombie Mom — Barry Burgess
$16.95

Letting Go: Collected Poems 1983-2003 — Donna Lisle Burton
$14.95
Way Past Time for Reflecting
$17.95

Gabriel's Songbook — Michael Amos Cody
$17.95

Musical Morphine: Transforming Pain One Note at a Time — Robin Russell Gaiser
$17.95 Finalist, USA Book Awards for Health: Alternative Medicine, 2017
Open for Lunch
$17.95 available Fall 2018

rhythms on a flaming drum — Michael Hopping
$16.95

I Like It Here! Adventures in the Wild & Wonderful World of Theatre — C. Robert Jones
$30.00

LANKY TALES — C. Robert Jones
Lanky Tales, Vol. I: The Bird Man & other stories
$9.00
Lanky Tales, Vol. II: Billy Red Wing & other stories
$9.00
Lanky Tales, Vol. III: A Good and Faithful Friend & other stories
$9.00
The Mystery at Claggett Cove
$9.00

Red-state, White-guy Blues — Jeff Douglas Messer
$15.95

Reed's Homophones: a comprehensive book of sound-alike words — A. D. Reed
$14.95 2018 sponsor of NPR's *Says You!*

Swords in their Hands: George Washington and the Newburgh Conspiracy — Dave Richards
$24.95 Finalist, USA Book Award for History 2014

Trang Sen: A Novel of Vietnam — Sarah-Ann Smith
$19.50

Invasive Procedures: Earthqukes, Calamities, & poems from the midst of life — Nan Socolow
$17.95

Deadly Dancing — THE RICK RYDER MYSTERY SERIES — RF Wilson
$15.95
Killer Weed
$14.95
The Pot Professor available Winter 2019
$15.95

Pisgah Press, LLC
PO Box 9663, Asheville, NC 28815-0663
www.pisgahpress.com

www.ingramcontent.com/pod-product-compliance
Lightning Source LLC
Chambersburg PA
CBHW052053110526
44591CB00013B/2197